NURTURING
Healing
LOVE

NURTURING
Healing
LOVE

| a Mother's Journey of Hope and Forgiveness | Scarlett Lewis

WITH
NATASHA Stoynoff |

HAY HOUSE

Carlsbad, California • New York City • London • Sydney
Johannesburg • Vancouver • Hong Kong • New Delhi

First published and distributed in the United Kingdom by:
Hay House UK Ltd, Astley House, 33 Notting Hill Gate, London W11 3JQ
Tel. +44 (0)20 3675 2450; Fax: +44 (0)20 3675 2451
www.hayhouse.co.uk

Published and distributed in the United States of America by:
Hay House Inc., PO Box 5100, Carlsbad, CA 92018-5100
Tel: (1) 760 431 7695 or (800) 654 5126
Fax: (1) 760 431 6948 or (800) 650 5115
www.hayhouse.com

Published and distributed in Australia by:
Hay House Australia Ltd, 18/36 Ralph St, Alexandria NSW 2015
Tel: (61) 2 9669 4299; Fax: (61) 2 9669 4144
www.hayhouse.com.au

Published and distributed in the Republic of South Africa by:
Hay House SA (Pty) Ltd, PO Box 990, Witkoppen 2068
Tel/Fax: (27) 11 467 8904
www.hayhouse.co.za

Published and distributed in India by:
Hay House Publishers India, Muskaan Complex, Plot No.3, B-2,
Vasant Kunj, New Delhi 110 070
Tel: (91) 11 4176 1620; Fax: (91) 11 4176 1630
www.hayhouse.co.in

Distributed in Canada by:
Raincoast, 9050 Shaughnessy St, Vancouver BC V6P 6E5
Tel: (1) 604 323 7100; Fax: (1) 604 323 2600

A catalogue record for this book is available from the British Library.

ISBN: 978-1-78180-177-2

Printed and bound in Great Britain by TJ International Ltd, Padstow, Cornwall.

MIX
Paper from
responsible sources
FSC   FSC® C013056
www.fsc.org

LOVINGLY DEDICATED TO MY TWO SONS,
J.T. AND JESSE, WHOM I LOVE WITH ALL
MY HEART; ONE MY ANGEL ON EARTH,
THE OTHER MY ANGEL IN HEAVEN.

Hanging with the boys in mom's hammock on Mother's Day, 2010

contents

FOREWORD *by Dr. Wayne W. Dyer* · ix
PREFACE *by Nick Ortner* · xv
INTRODUCTION: BORN BRAVE · xix

PART I: LIFE, LOVE, AND DEATH
CHAPTER 1: Here's Jesse! · 3
CHAPTER 2: December 14th · 11
CHAPTER 3: Light in the Darkness · 27
CHAPTER 4: Sacred Grieving · 37

PART II: SIGNS
CHAPTER 5: Hearts to Heaven · 45
CHAPTER 6: Energies and Messages · 53
CHAPTER 7: Jesse in the Sky with Jesus · 63

PART III: HEALING
CHAPTER 8: Nurturing a Foundation · 77
CHAPTER 9: Sharing and Forgiving · 89
CHAPTER 10: Trauma and Looking Within · 99

PART IV: MOVING FORWARD
CHAPTER 11: Helping Hands · 111
CHAPTER 12: Finding a Voice for Change · 125
CHAPTER 13: Message to the World · 137

EPILOGUE: LOVE NEVER ENDS · 145
ACKNOWLEDGMENTS · 151
ABOUT THE AUTHORS · 157
ABOUT THE FOUNDATION · 159

Foreword | BY DR. WAYNE W. DYER

I didn't read this book. I felt it. I felt every word, every sentence, every paragraph, every page, every chapter, right up through the end—when Scarlett thanks her precious little boy for teaching her the greatest lesson of this life: love never ends.

The penetrating and thoughtful book you hold in your hands brought home to me, in a very big way, something the poet, spiritual teacher, and my friend Maya Angelou said when we were on a radio show in San Francisco many years ago. "I've learned," Maya said, "that people will forget what you said, will forget what you did, but people will never forget how you made them feel." I have never forgotten these words, though sometimes their truth hits me more forcefully.

Immersing myself in this book made me feel in a way that I will always remember. It made me feel a wide range of emotions from anger to frustration to sadness to despair to joy to appreciation for the endless miracles that surround us—and it made me feel hope, hope for a far better world. And finally, it made me feel love because the book you are about to *feel* is not a story of rage and revenge as one could well understand in the face of such a horrific experience as the one that took place at Sandy Hook Elementary School where Scarlett's little boy Jesse was senselessly murdered. No, this is truly a love story, a story that clearly sends the message that love itself never ends and that it is our destiny as a people to learn and apply this lesson even in the face of circumstances that are beyond comprehension.

When tragedy strikes, our first human response is to react in anger and with rage in our hearts, to attempt to end such dark behavior by throwing more darkness at the problem. Yet our rational minds tell us that reacting with darkness in the form of hatred and madness simply expands and multiplies the darkness. The only answer to so much darkness is to bring light. As Saint Francis of Assisi reminded us in his widely recited prayer, "Where there is darkness, let me bring light."

Scarlett, in writing this book and sharing the lessons of her bodhisattva son Jesse, is asking all of us to bring our own light to the omnipresence of darkness in our world. She asks us to see that love itself is the way forward, reiterating what Jesus taught us: "But I say to you, love your enemies and pray for those who persecute you." This is the only solution to the kind of darkness that brings such violence.

Scarlett Lewis has faced the ultimate darkness. She has shared, from a deep place of truth within, the agony of losing her Jesse at such a tender age. She has shared her very personal journey back to living and teaching how to become instruments of love.

Jesse Lewis is here among us. He communicates regularly with his mom to keep her on a path of love. He came to Scarlett as a bundle of love, and his few short years here among us were all about fun, laughter, excitement, joy, gratitude, and yes, love. It was the very last message Jesse scrawled in the frost on his mother's car window on the day he reclaimed his place with God, the place that is defined as love: "God is love. Whoever lives in love, lives in God and God in him." (1 John 4:16) In fact, it was words he left for Scarlett that comprise the title of this book: *Nurturing Healing Love.* These words illuminate how this young boy lived a life of Christ consciousness right up until his last breath. He sought to share his happiness, to have fun, and to glory in the natural gifts provided for all of us.

Jesse's life is a model for us, and Scarlett's courageous sharing of this story is Jesse's gift to her and to all of us who strive to shift our planet and our people once and for all out of the darkness of hatred, fear, and inhumanity. The great lesson of this book is that love never dies. How can it? It is formless; therefore, it has no beginning and no end. There is something deathless that lives in every one of God's creations. It is eternal. It is our source of being. It is spirit. Jesse is right here, right now with me as I write these words and as Scarlett goes about living her transformed life as a teacher of this divine love. This is her new mission, to teach us all that it is possible to change an angry thought to love just as Saint Francis beseeched God in his prayer, "Lord, make me an instrument of thy peace. Where there is hatred, let me sow love." This is our ultimate calling. This is what we must learn if we are to survive and thrive as a people. This is our greatest challenge, to put aside our egos and to embrace compassion and love.

As the poet William Wordsworth reminded us, "Our birth is but a sleep and a forgetting . . . Heaven lies about us in our infancy." A young child named Jesse Lewis came to us and showed us that Earth really is crammed with heaven, and he left his mother an assignment to live and teach love even in the most abominable of situations. Jesse is there giving his mama clues that she can always choose love. He is with her even now, fulfilling his own dharma to bring the light of love to the world, to help people realize that they can choose to change an angry thought to one of lovingkindness. I once heard the Dalai Lama say that if we took each child at the age of eight and taught him to meditate, we could end, in one generation, the hatred and violence that is so much a part of our lives. This is the power of love and the power of Jesse's message.

One of the greatest lessons of my own life was learning to turn the inner rampage of hatred and anger toward my own father for the reprehensible behavior and abandonment of his family into an inner reaction more closely aligned with God and God-realized love. I came to understand that he was one of my greatest teachers, and that he played a part in helping me do the work I was destined to do. He gave me the opportunity to practice turning hostile thoughts into thoughts of forgiveness and love.

Loss and hurt make for a strange and painful journey indeed, as Scarlett knows so well and writes about from a divine place of truth and passion. She has come to know and teach the eternal truth that whatever the problem, no matter how severe, love is the answer. This is the message of all of our great spiritual masters.

They taught that enlightenment does not bring love; rather love itself is what brings enlightenment. As the 16th-century metaphysical Christian mystic known as Saint John of the Cross once reminded his followers, "Where there is no love, put love, and you will find love." This is Jesse's instruction to Scarlett and to all of us as well. And this is precisely what I felt as Scarlett's poignant words infused me throughout my reading of this beautifully honest book.

It is an honor and a privilege to have shared the stage with Scarlett in New York, as she brought the audience to its feet in a thunderous cacophony of applause. Her message is a reflection of Jesse's life. It is what I humbly attempt to live and teach. Where there is hatred, change the thought. Where there is no love, we must put love, and then surely we will find love. I love you, Jesse. After devouring every word of this book, I too feel your spirit guiding me as it guides your amazing mama.

I AM,
Wayne Dyer

preface | BY NICK ORTNER

From the moment I met Scarlett Lewis, I felt that something was different about her. As a fellow resident of Newtown, Connecticut, I had spent the previous month and a half, with my colleague Dr. Lori Leyden, meeting one on one and in small groups with residents who had been affected by the horrific shootings at Sandy Hook Elementary school. We were teaching them how to use a technique called EFT, or simply *Tapping*, to help them process the deep trauma and stress they were experiencing.

When Dr. Leyden and I walked into Scarlett's house on a drizzly Tuesday evening in January, I wasn't sure what to expect. The people we had been working with were deeply traumatized, as would be expected from such a tragic event. Just as you would imagine, the closer a person was to the tragedy, the more painful it was and the more deeply they were hurt. And while I could see a terrible pain within Scarlett, the deep grief of having lost her precious Jesse, there was also something else there. It was clear that her pain had not overtaken the part of her that knows there is more to this world than meets the eye. This part of her was still alive, whispering words of hope, love, compassion, forgiveness, and healing, even during the most profound depths of her grief.

These whispers are what inspired this book. It is the deeper part of Scarlett that wrote this book, and it is that part of you to which this book speaks. It opens your eyes to the deeper levels of being, and it has the potential to change your life.

On the very first evening I met Scarlett, she shared with me many of the stories you're about to read. She showed me the pictures, showed me the chalkboard, showed me the drawings and notes and bits and pieces that all called out and said, "Love Never Ends." And it was in the recounting of these tales and ideas that I could see her compassion, love, and forgiveness, which are hard to find in this world and even harder to find so soon after such a painful and tragic event.

Since that night, I've had the opportunity to get to know Scarlett, to continue to work with her on healing the trauma of that day, the wounds of the loss, and the stress of a new life; and through all of it, I've had the chance to watch her heal. I've been able to witness her forgiving even more, loving even more, and inspiring even more. I've seen her lift the spirits of 50 people at a small gathering, and I've seen her move thousands to their feet.

I believe Scarlett has the power to do this because she truly believes that there is more to this world than meets the eye. The whispering voice of love, healing, compassion, and forgiveness speaks more loudly to her. And it shows itself in the pages you are about to read. Soak in this tale, full of tragedy and full of hope, full of darkness and full of light, and allow it to seep into your soul. Allow it to help you heal your own wounds and to approach the world in a different way. Let it inspire you to nurture more, to heal more, and to love more.

Listen and take in Jesse's message to us all: "Nurturing Healing Love."

— Nick Ortner

INTRODUCTION — Born Brave

Jesse was born brave.

Maybe if he hadn't been quite so brave, I might still be singing my wake-up song to my precious six-year-old each morning. And maybe if he hadn't been quite so courageous he would be here to blow out the seven candles I'll be lighting on his next birthday cake.

But Jesse was who he was—a first grader with a happy, ever-ready grin whom God had given a warrior's heart. He was only four feet tall, but he feared very little and never backed away from a challenge or from doing what he thought was right, be it climbing into the saddle of a horse that towered over him or stepping up to help someone in danger. Jesse had an old soul, and despite his tender years, he seemed to know that choosing to love in all we do makes the world a better place.

So, although heartbroken, I wasn't surprised to learn from police investigators that when the first blasts of automatic gunfire echoed through the hallways of Sandy Hook Elementary School last December, Jesse didn't run. And when Miss Soto, the first-grade teacher he loved so dearly, tried to hide the children in the bathroom and in different areas of the classroom, Jesse remained by her side.

Jesse stayed by his teacher even when the armed gunman, a mentally disturbed 20-year-old, walked into the classroom and opened fire. No one is entirely certain of the exact order of events that occurred in the ensuing minutes, but it is very likely that a bullet fragment from one of the shots that killed Miss Soto grazed the side of Jesse's head, yet didn't take him down.

The kids who survived reported that even with this head wound, Jesse stayed on his feet and faced the gunman. And it was then that Jesse did what I am now certain he was put on this earth to do: he saved lives. When something happened to the shooter's gun and he was forced to stop for a moment, either to fix it or to reload, Jesse yelled to his classmates that this was their chance to escape. He shouted for them to run, to run as fast as they could, to run *now!* And they did. They listened to Jesse and ran for their lives. Nine terrified first graders managed to run from the classroom to safety as the gunman took aim at Jesse. Then he shot my son in the forehead and finished what he'd come to do: kill as many innocent people in the school as he could. He killed 26 in all, 20 children and 6 adults. When the first responders arrived on the scene they found Jesse's lifeless body on the floor next to the body of Miss Soto.

That single act of anger and violence on December 14, 2012, shocked the world and plunged the idyllic village of Sandy Hook into despair. And it left the parents and family members who lost children and other loved ones that day to endure a grief so grueling and

Jesse was King of the Pumpkin Patch, Halloween 2012

profound, a life sentence of sorrow and suffering so insurmountable, that surviving the heartache seemed impossible.

But this is not a story about a massacre, although that is how my journey begins.

It is a story about how we can face, endure, and survive the seemingly impossible, and find courage when we think we have none. It's about choosing love instead of anger, fear, or hatred, and standing our ground, like Jesse did. And it's about how all these choices can change your life and even the world we live in. That is why I chose to write this book—to share with you a message that Jesse shared with me: through nurturing, healing love we can mend our hearts and enrich our world.

Although my story has many moments of sorrow, it's not a sad story—it's a love story. It's about my love for my sons, my family, my community, and God.

So please bear with me through the difficult times because, after the tears, most of all, this is a mother's journey of hope, healing, destiny, and even miracles.

In my darkest hours following the tragedy, my son Jesse reached out from heaven to give me signs that he is still with me every minute of every day. And in doing so, he's taught me anew the everlasting and beautiful truth I first taught him as a child: love never ends.

PART I
Life, LOVE, AND DEATH

CHAPTER
ONE

Here's Jesse!

Jesse McCord Lewis came into this world the same way he would live each day of his life—like a force of nature.

He was born on June 30, 2006, weighing in at a whopping 11 pounds and with an ear-jarring set of lungs. From the get-go he was in a rush to tackle life. On my first visit to the nursery I was surprised to find a group of nurses gathered around Jesse's crib, oohing and aahing and taking photos. It seems Jesse had tried to crawl out of his bassinet before he was even one day old. "I've never seen that happen in all my years in the maternity ward," said one nurse, shaking her head in amazement.

As he got older, Jesse was still in a hurry, and never grew tired of making big entrances. Why walk into a room when you could run in with arms spread wide, yelling "*Heeeerrre's Jesse!*"? He had a big personality and a big voice to match. He was named after his grandfather and great-grandfather, Jesse and McCord. I chose the name because it sounded rough-and-tumble to me, like a cowboy.

A few people thought Jesse was a bit too noisy and overactive, but to me, especially in hindsight, I believe

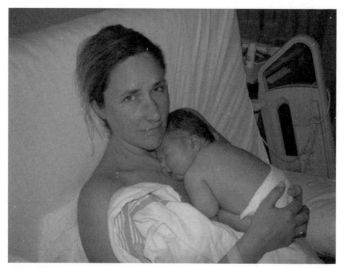

Big entrance: my Sweet Boy of Joy weighs in at a whopping 11 pounds, with a personality to match

Jesse was in such a lively hurry because he had an intuitive sense that he would only have a short time on this planet.

I must have sensed that as well. On the day he was born, I held Jesse in my arms and said this prayer:

> Dear Jesus, thank you so much for Jesse. I know that he is a gift, and I know that you could take him from me at any time, but please don't.

I don't know where that prayer came from or why I said it, but I said it every night of his life after tucking him in to sleep. I'd slip my hand under his pajama top and rest it on his chest to feel his beating heart, and I'd say the Jesse Prayer. Looking back, the prayer was just one of countless signs I believe

God sent to prepare me for the unimaginably painful event in my future.

I didn't know it then, but I had been preparing for this event for years. Before Jesse was born I'd written and published a story about a mother and a child having to part. I wrote *Rose's Foal*, a children's book, after 9/11 when my older son and only other child, J.T. (Joseph Theodore), was just one year old. I wanted to share a story of hope and beauty with J.T. as he grew older. I didn't want his imagination to be filled with the images of violence and death that had become such a part of our daily lives. We had recently moved to a small farm in Connecticut that we still call home today, so I decided to use the natural surroundings of our farm for inspiration. I'd always loved horses and had ridden since I was a child; we had several of our own at the farm. The day before the attacks, our horse Rose gave birth to a baby colt.

Over the next few months, I would put J.T. in his little red Radio Flyer wagon and pull him out to the barn to take photos of Rose and her colt. Later I wrote a simple story about a mother horse teaching her colt about love, being brave, and loss. The mare explains that sometimes a mother and child must separate and "one day they might not live on the same farm." But even if they never saw each other again, they would always be together in their hearts.

"Every mother and child share a special bond in their hearts, regardless of distance or time, forever and always," the mare reassures her colt, because "love never ends."

J.T. loved that book, and years later Jesse would

come to love it, too—he asked me to read it to him over and over again.

Another thing I now realize was part of my unknown journey to prepare for this event was my quest to become the best mom and person I could be.

Like so many people, while growing up I accumulated my share of anxieties and fears that stayed with me into adulthood. I often lived my life and made decisions from a place of fear and worry—fear about the future and worry about losing what I had. This pattern kept me trapped in a cycle of emotional turmoil that among other things lead me into some unhealthy relationships. And even though my own parents' divorce had been devastating to me when I was a teenager, I ended up as a single mom.

I had a lot of baggage in my life, but by the time Jesse was born, I'd decided to make changes so I could set a good example for my kids and be a better person for myself. I set out on a spiritual journey, which began with widening my traditional belief system. I was raised Episcopalian, and I held on to my routine of daily prayer and Bible reading. But when I decided to change, I opened myself up to new ideas and methods—how to heal myself and contemplate the world in ways that might raise eyebrows in my hometown of Fayetteville, Arkansas.

I surrounded myself with new mentors, learned new concepts, and read mind-expanding books. One in particular inspired me to take my journey to the next step. Louise Hay's *You Can Heal Your Life* opened my eyes to the power of positive thinking and officially launched my lifelong exploration of other inspirational books—be they the words of Wayne Dyer,

Deepak Chopra, or Eckhart Tolle. This obsession with reading inspirational literature often made me the object of the boys' friendly teasing.

"Oh, Mom! We don't wanna hear it!" J.T. would say, rolling his eyes, when I tried to teach them about positive affirmations or mind over matter or whatever else I was studying at the time.

"Yeah, Mom," Jesse would chime in. "It's a choice, it's a choice, *it's a choice* . . . we get it!"

And while they chided me and laughed at what I was doing, they truly did get the benefit of everything I learned. I felt gratitude for the blessings in my life, and I promised myself that I would never pass up an opportunity to kiss my boys or tell them "I love you."

I can still remember the first time I put that thought into action as I passed by Jesse's crib one night on my way to make a work call. I caught a glimpse of his soft little cheek, and my internal monologue went like this: *Oh, what a sweet cheek! But I have to make a call . . . I'll kiss it later. Wait, no. Do not pass up this moment. These moments are gifts. You never know when you will get another opportunity to kiss that little cheek.*

So I put off the call for a few minutes and kissed his cheek, and from that kiss onward I grabbed every chance I got to express my love and affection to my boys. And thank God I did.

Over the next six years, Jesse grew into a delightful combination of a lovable mama's boy who couldn't cuddle enough and a fearless, rambunctious kid who was all boy. He'd bound downstairs and streak through the kitchen like a comet to get outside and play soccer, stomp through the mud, swing from tree branches, chase the dogs, and jump off the highest hay bale. He loved birds of all kinds; he checked out library books on birding and had a pair of yellow binoculars he'd roam around the farm with, trying to identify as many different species as he could. And like his mama, he loved to paint. Whenever he joined me in my art room upstairs where I was often working on portraits of the boys, we joked that I became his attentive assistant—replenishing his colors and rinsing his brushes—as he focused on his art.

At night, he'd climb into his bubble bath and surround himself with dozens of colorful little rubber ducks of every variety—cowboy ducks, sailor ducks, ducks with sombreros, superhero ducks, football player ducks, military ducks, and so on—by lining them up along the rim of the tub. He'd coo to them and care for them as though they were living creatures. And then he'd shift straight into playing war with his prized collection of toy soldiers that he called "army men." Rubber duckies and army men were scattered all over the house and yard—it was a sweet dichotomy that really captured Jesse's personality.

In keeping with his gentle spirit, his affinity for soldiers was more with the United Nations–type peacekeeper than the Schwarzenegger commando–type warrior. That's just who Jesse was. God gave him a protective spirit. He loved going on "patrol" around the farm. He'd put on his green army helmet, and slip on his heavy snow boots with a camouflage design—even in the blazing summer heat—because they looked like combat boots. Then he'd tuck a plastic water pistol in the waistband of his shorts and off he'd go, marching

Peacekeeper: Jesse on patrol at home, wearing his camouflage army helmet

around the perimeter of our property then posting himself at the front gate, where he'd stand on guard until sunset. I loved watching him from the kitchen window, knowing how happy it made him to protect the home front and keep us safe.

But I think my favorite times with Jesse were the mornings.

First, I'd wake him up with a song:

I woke up this morning with an angel in my bed,
he must have been trying to rest his precious head.
He said, Could I bother you for something to eat,
and I said, Yes, angels love something very sweet.

The corners of his mouth would curl into a smile, and then I'd kiss his cheek and start tickling him. A minute later he'd be fully awake and ready to rumble. "Let's wrestle!" he'd shout.

We'd roll on the bed wrestling, hugging, and tickling until one of us begged for mercy or it was time to start the day. One of my fondest morning memories is from a day last fall when our regular tickle session had gone on longer than usual.

"Okay, Jesse, we have to go, I have to leave for work . . ."

My head was in Jesse's lap, and he started to stroke my forehead and hair.

"Mama . . . Mama . . . Mama . . ." he whispered over and over again.

I looked up at him and thought, *If I don't go now, I'm going to be late for work. But this moment is heaven; it's perfection. I want to be here and nowhere else. I never want it to end.*

I was a little late that day.

December 14th

My last morning with Jesse began like so many others; I woke him up with a song, kissed him until he giggled, and we wrestled until time tore us apart. Neil, Jesse's father, was picking Jesse up to take him to school that day, and Jesse was scheduled to spend the night at his dad's house. I wasn't going to see him until the next afternoon, when Neil and I would join him in his classroom to build gingerbread houses.

It was a bright, beautiful, sunny morning, but so cold that my car and everything else in the yard was coated with a layer of frost. I bundled Jesse into his coat and gloves, and we headed outside. While Jesse walked toward the car, I chatted with Neil to finalize our plans to meet at Jesse's school. Since we'd split, our relationship had been strained at times, but we did our best to get along for Jesse's sake.

When I turned to kiss Jesse good-bye, I saw him standing beside my car with an ear-to-ear grin. He'd written a note to me in the frost on the passenger-side window and door—*I Love You.* He'd etched little hearts all around the sweet words, and now he stood there smiling up at me.

"Wait there, Jesse, don't move!" I pleaded with him, and ran to get my camera. I was going to be late for work, but I simply had to get a photo! And I did—Jesse grinning in the blinding sunlight beside the love poem that would be his good-bye note to his mama.

I kissed his cheek and made sure his seat belt was fastened before Neil drove away with him.

The next day I awoke at dawn, as I always do, and I said my usual morning prayer before opening my eyes: "Thank you for my boys, Lord, and for our farm, for our health, for our family and friends . . . and for us all being together . . ."

As I began my day, I noticed how quiet the house was. When Jesse was gone, it was markedly more silent. His presence was so big and he was so loud, it was like living with a percussionist who never took a rest. That's why one of my favorite nicknames for him was Bingo Bango Bongo Drum; my other favorite was Sweet Boy of Joy, because that's what he was to me.

I began my daily morning routine, waiting with J.T. for his 6:30 A.M. school bus, then feeding the horses, chickens, and dogs. After the chores, I sat at the kitchen table with a mug of coffee and inspected a gift I'd recently received from a friend.

It was a twine necklace with an unusual silver cross made of diachronic glass flecked with green, blue, gold, and Jesse's favorite color—"turk boys" (turquoise). It was a bit too large and showy to go with the conservative business suit I wore to the office, and whenever I wore a cross it was always my grandmother's understated silver one. But the more I examined

December 13th: The last time I saw him alive, Jesse wrote me a love note.

this one, the more I was struck by its beauty and by the special meaning it held coming to me at that particular moment in our lives.

Jesse, J.T., and I had just begun attending church together on a regular basis. The inspiration came on a Saturday evening after a family gathering where the boys' behavior had been unusually rowdy, unruly, and argumentative all day. We'd left the family event early, and when their ill-behaved attitudes continued in the car on the way home, I realized something had to change.

"You know, boys, we are having a hard time and we need something," I announced, watching them in the rearview mirror. "And do you know what that *something* is that we need? We need *God*. Tomorrow, we're going to church."

I'd attended church fairly regularly as a child, but as an adult my churchgoing had become sporadic even though my faith was strong. I taught my boys the tenets of the Golden Rule—always doing unto others as you'd have them do unto you. And we spent many evenings reading Bible stories together, particularly the Gospels that stressed the importance of practicing love, faith, charity, kindness, compassion, and forgiveness. We'd made prayer a part of our lives and prayed often at home. But, as the boys got older, I felt there was still something missing in our spiritual lives.

So the very next morning we were sitting in a pew at Beacon Hill Evangelical Free Church, which had been recommended by my neighbor and friend Roberta. The boys grumbled a bit at first, but soon they looked forward to going. I remember in particular how excited Jesse had been after seeing a video about the life of Jesus in Sunday school—"He gave up his life to save everyone else?" Jesse asked, incredulous. He also loved reading about young King David's fight with the armored giant, Goliath.

"Mom . . . even though he was smaller and only had a slingshot, David was able to defeat the giant and save his people because he was smarter and had faith!" Jesse said, excitedly. I smiled, wondering if Jesse would imagine himself as the brave young David the next time he pulled on his little "army" snow boots and helmet to guard our front gate.

So all of that was running through my mind as I sat in the kitchen examining my pretty new cross necklace. *Yes,* I thought. *Not quite sure why, but today's your day.* I slipped it around my neck and headed out to the office.

As I was driving to work, Neil was driving Jesse to Sandy Hook Elementary School. Although Neil and I had finalized the plans to meet at Jesse's classroom later that day, Jesse was worried about what was going to happen. He was certain that it wasn't going to work out, and he was uncharacteristically melancholy.

"Don't worry, Jess, Mom and I will be there," Neil said.

"No," Jesse answered, "it's not going to happen."

Neil was surprised by Jesse's reaction—it was an odd way for Jesse to talk. "Of course it is going to happen, Jess. It's all arranged."

"No," Jesse repeated, shaking his head. "It's not going to happen, Dad."

When they got to the school, Neil parked the car and walked with Jesse through the front doors and into the main hallway, where they hugged good-bye as usual.

"Dad?" Jesse said, putting his hands on Neil's shoulders as they came out of the hug. "I just want you to know . . . it's going to be okay. And that I love you and Mom."

Then Jesse turned and walked away down the hall toward his first-grade classroom.

As Jesse was saying good-bye to his dad, I was just arriving at my office at the software communications company where I'd been working as an executive assistant to the CEO for almost a year. I'd acquired a bit of a reputation as the office Pollyanna because I'd papered my cubicle with empowering messages and inspirational quotes on Post-it notes. I'd been at my desk for about an hour when my colleague Tina sent me an instant message: DID YOU HEAR ABOUT A SHOOTING AT A SCHOOL IN NEWTOWN?

The message startled me, but I remained calm. Even if the report were true, what were the odds that of all the schools in Newtown, something like that would happen at Jesse's or J.T.'s? I'd begun to IM Tina back when my phone rang.

"Scarlett?" It was my friend and neighbor Diane, and she sounded worried. "Did you hear that a teacher got shot in the foot at Jesse's school?"

A second later, every electronic device around me was ringing, beeping, or vibrating, delivering a barrage of phone calls, texts, e-mails, and IMs from family, friends, and colleagues. Everybody was either asking me what was going on or giving me fragments of information they'd heard. It was too much for my brain to assemble, but it seemed clear that there had been a shooting, and it had definitely happened at Sandy Hook Elementary . . . *Jesse's school!*

I took a deep breath and told myself to stay calm. There'd been a false report about a school shooting in town before; maybe this was another one of those.

Then Neil called, worried.

"Nothing really bad could have happened, Neil. This is Sandy Hook! What could happen here? Jesse is *fine*. Nothing could ever happen to him. *Ever! It's just not possible.*"

Neil was heading out to pick up Jesse at the Sandy Hook firehouse, which had been designated as the official meeting place for parents and students. I decided I would just go as well, in case Jesse needed consoling. Within 15 minutes of getting that first instant message from Tina, I was in my car and on my way to the firehouse. En route I pulled up to the farm, ran inside, grabbed my grandmother's silver cross necklace, slipped it around my neck, and jumped back behind the wheel.

Sandy Hook Elementary is nestled in a wooded enclave at the end of a mile-long road that branches off from a main village thoroughfare and dead-ends at the school's parking lot, with nothing but trees in between. The firehouse sits on the main thoroughfare a mile away from the school, and by the time I reached town the roads were so clogged with emergency vehicles, television satellite trucks, and parents' cars that I had to park a few blocks away.

As I got out of my car I kept repeating the same mantra that had been looping through my mind since leaving work: *Jesse is fine, Jesse is just fine.* Nevertheless, I ran toward the firehouse.

When I got there I was greeted by mass confusion. Hundreds of panicked parents were wandering around shouting their kids' names, and bewildered and frightened kids cried out for their parents. Neil hadn't arrived yet. I entered the building alone and was immediately stopped by an official.

"If you haven't found your child yet, go to the back corner."

I stepped into the noise and commotion, wading through the sea of unclaimed children, scanning the faces for Jesse. When I didn't see him I began looking for one of his classmates, but I couldn't see any of those faces, either. I stood in the center of the fire-truck bay for a few seconds watching as one, then two, and then dozens of relieved moms and dads found their sons and daughters and snatched them up into their arms, hugging and kissing them and whispering, *Oh, thank God!*

As the parent-and-child reunions multiplied around me and the crowd began to thin out, I still could not see Jesse. I began approaching anyone wearing a uniform, anyone who looked in the least bit official. "I can't find my son; his name is Jesse," I said to at least a half dozen people. Each one had the same response: "Wait in the corner, ma'am . . . We're asking all the parents who can't find their kids to wait in the back room."

I stuck my head into the room. There were no kids, but there were plenty of worried parents trying frantically to get news, any news, on the whereabouts of their children. *To hell with this,* I thought. *Jesse's out there wandering around somewhere and he needs me.* When I turned back to the main hall, I spotted a police officer whom I had met years before when he had given a talk to J.T.'s first-grade class. I stopped him and asked for help.

I was sure he would have no idea who I was, but he said, "Sure I remember you, Scarlett." What a relief! Perhaps he could help. But he was being surrounded by other parents, all with the same question, and to each of us, he calmly said, "I'm sure everything's going to be fine. Just wait in the back room and keep clear of the media outside."

Someone I knew from Jesse's PTA had overheard my exchange with the police officer and tapped me on the shoulder, pointing to a pretty yellow house about 100 feet down the road. "Scarlett, I'm not positive," she said, "but I think Jesse and some of the other kids from his class ran into that house."

Oh, thank God.

Moments later I was banging on the door of the yellow house, but the soft-spoken, gray-haired man who answered said that a school bus driver had run to his house with six schoolchildren after the "incident," but a policeman had already picked them up.

"I think the officer took them to the day care down the hill, on the other side of the firehouse—you should try looking for him over there."

Oh, thank God.

Neil called as I was heading back down the hill. I told him to check the day care, and I'd go back to the firehouse. But before I returned I decided to walk straight up the road toward the school; maybe Jesse was waiting for me there at the front door. Military personnel in fatigues were patrolling the wooded drive, and I didn't make it more than 20 feet before I was stopped. They were turning back everyone who approached the school. There was noise and activity all around me, and when I looked up I saw police helicopters circling the grounds just overhead. Several jeeps and Humvees carrying soldiers armed with machine guns and flash grenades drove past me, waved through by the guards. I thought of how excited Jesse would be to see real-life army men, and then wondered why on earth such a large military presence was needed.

Jesse is fine, Jesse is just fine, I kept repeating, as I approached several guards to describe Jesse and ask if they'd seen my boy. I got the same answers from every official I spoke to: "No," "Don't know," or "Parents looking for children are to wait in the firehouse and not talk to the media, ma'am."

Neil texted: HE'S NOT AT THE DAY-CARE CENTER. NOW WHAT?

What else could we do? I told him I was going back to the firehouse. By that time, my mother, Maureen, her husband, Bob, and my friend Diane had arrived. Two of my brothers who lived in the state were on their way by car. When J.T. texted and asked if he could join us, I told him OKAY. *I want the three of us together,* I thought. *Once we find Jesse, we can all go home, reunited, as a family.*

The atmosphere in the firehouse had become increasingly tense. Hundreds of children had already been reunited with their parents and left for home, and those of us who remained were frightened and frustrated and demanding answers—loudly. A state trooper moved from one group of parents to the next, trying to calm nerves.

"We're sweeping and resweeping the school," he said. "Some of the children went to hide in bathrooms and closets. So we are looking in every corner and crevice of the building to find them. They might not know it's safe now and are still too frightened to come out.

Some kids may have even run out of the school and are hiding in the woods. Our search teams are combing the woods right now."

Of course! Jesse's so scrappy and resourceful that he's hiding someplace nobody would think to look. He's still hiding there now; he's just so smart that they haven't been able to find him yet!

Then the trooper asked me for a description of the clothes Jesse was wearing that day and for a recent picture of him. I gave him the details as I checked my phone for photos. Another officer came to get Jesse's full name to add him to the list of children who were yet to be located.

By early afternoon we still hadn't been given any information from officials on what exactly had happened inside the school or if any of our children were hurt. Parents were swapping unconfirmed news reports and rumors—like there was a second gunman at large, which panicked people even more. We had no idea what to think, what had gone on, where our babies were, or what was going to happen next.

Somebody ordered food, and delivery guys appeared with dozens of pizzas, but I can't remember seeing anyone eat—I certainly couldn't. At that point all I could do was wait and huddle with my family. J.T. had arrived, and I hugged him as tightly as I could and told him the same words I'd been repeating all day— not to worry, Jesse was fine.

I was strong. I had hope. I had to. At least, part of me did—the part that had been denying what was happening since Tina's first message that morning, the part that wouldn't even entertain the thought that any harm could ever come to Jesse. Another part of me subconsciously knew Jesse was gone. I have absolutely no memory of this, but my friend Pam and several other friends told me later that when they texted me throughout the afternoon asking for an update on Jesse, I texted the reply JESSE IS WITH JESUS. Deep down I knew, as I had known would happen from the moment Jesse was born and I first said the Jesse Prayer over his little body in the hospital, that God had taken back the precious gift he had given me.

And then the screaming started.

One of the parents at the opposite side of the room made a sound that cut my heart in two, expressing a loss that words can't define. The sounds of human anguish echoed through the hall. Hearing them, J.T. winced, as though he'd been struck, so I got up and ushered him outside to the back of the firehouse. This is where Neil had been most of the day, talking to officials and trying to get updates. He came over to us and pulled me aside.

"Scarlett, my mother died five years ago on this very day. Jesse was asking me about her last week. He was worried about how he'd recognize her in heaven if he died. I told him that I'd be in heaven well before him and that I'd meet him and introduce him to her. Scarlett, if Jesse is dead, what does all that mean?"

The thought of Jesse being dead was the last thing I wanted to talk about or even acknowledge the possibility of, but I could see that Neil was seeking comfort and reassurance.

"I guess it means . . . it was a gift for you, Neil—a message from your mother that she would be in heaven to meet him."

Another scream rose up behind us. It was too much; I was hyperfocused on J.T., and I had to get him as far away from the trauma as I could to protect him. By then most of my family members who lived nearby had joined us at the firehouse—my mom and Bob, and my brothers Trent and Jordan and their wives. My other brother, Coulter, and his wife were on their way from Boston, and my father and his wife, Beth, were on their way from Arkansas.

"Please, guys, let's move," I said. "I want peace. Whatever is going to happen, I want peace around us."

We moved into the parking lot but had to keep going farther and farther away every time a grim-faced official approached another family with news that triggered an outburst of grief too painful and loud to ignore. But no matter how much distance I put between us and that firehouse, the truth kept getting nearer. I looked into my heart and began to accept the possibility that Jesse might be gone. I said to myself that if—and that was only if—something bad had happened, if Jesse had been "taken" from us, then he'd been taken while he was doing something brave, something good, something courageous.

I thought, *Jesse was born brave, that is who he is. If he's not coming back to me it's because he was protecting Miss Soto or his friends. It's who he is. I can feel it. If he's not coming back, that is what happened.*

Someone brought out folding lawn chairs for us to sit on, and we all slumped into them, emotionally and physically exhausted from the day. I sat down across from J.T. and pulled my chair toward him until our knees were touching. I took his face in my hands.

"J.T., even if the worst has happened and we've

lost Jesse, we know exactly where he is, and we know he is fine. It's going to be okay."

"No, it's not, Mom . . . How can you say that? It is not going to be okay . . ."

"Yes, it *is* going to be okay. If Jesse is gone then he is with Jesus in heaven, and that's a place more wonderful than we can even imagine. If he was badly hurt inside of the school today then he is not in pain anymore; he is in perfect health and he's happy now because he's in heaven."

J.T. shook his head, tears streaming down his cheeks.

"No, no, no. It is not going to be okay, it is not going to be okay, it is never going to be okay!"

"It absolutely is, J.T., and we are *absolutely* going to be fine."

I kept repeating that we would be fine, as I had kept repeating that Jesse was going to be fine. I clutched my grandmother's cross with my hand and drew on my faith for strength—I knew what I was saying was true. The family adjusted their chairs to form a circle so we could all face one another. And then we sat silently and waited. An hour passed, maybe two.

In the late afternoon an elderly doctor crossed the parking lot and headed in our direction. It was our turn. The doctor walked straight to me and knelt down on one knee at the side of my chair.

"There is no easy way to say this. Your son is dead."

I stared at him and said nothing; I couldn't. At that moment, I couldn't feel, I couldn't move, I couldn't cry. Not until J.T. began sobbing, and then I threw my arms around him and hugged him as hard as I could.

"It is going to be okay, J.T. I promise."

The rest of my family encircled us with their arms, and we held one another tightly.

My brother Coulter and his wife, Kristy, arrived at the firehouse soon after, and my mother left our circle to meet them in the parking lot. Even from that distance, I knew exactly when she'd told them Jesse was dead because Coulter doubled over.

I also saw Neil in the parking lot, standing alone, crying. I kissed J.T. and went over to Neil. Our relationship had been difficult, but he was Jesse's father, and we had both just lost our precious, precious son. We looked at each other and hugged without speaking, then we parted, and I walked back to my family.

I didn't want to think about what had happened. I didn't want to think about tomorrow or how I'd feel when I woke up without Jesse in the house. I didn't want to think about how I would have to do that every day for the rest of my life.

I didn't want to think or feel anything at that moment; all I wanted was my family's strong arms around me so I wouldn't collapse. As I crossed the parking lot, I scanned the scene and took in the remains of the day—the sobbing families, the soldiers armed with grenades, the media's bright television lights shining on all of us.

"Let's go home," I said, when I got back to our little circle of chairs. "There is nothing left for us here."

CHAPTER
THREE

Light
in the
Darkness

The next morning I awoke in the predawn dark and instinctively reached out to stroke Jesse's hair in case he'd slipped into bed next to me, whispering the first words of my morning prayer to thank God for all my blessings. A few seconds later, I realized I was not at home but at my mother's house, and Jesse was not beside me. The prayer died on my lips.

Reality hit me like a kick in the stomach. My gut twisted into knots so painful that my knees jerked to my chest and I rolled into a fetal position. I slapped my hand over my mouth so I wouldn't vomit into the sheets. For a few desperate seconds my mind clutched at hope—*I didn't see his body, nobody showed us a body . . . the doctor got it wrong, it's just a big mistake . . . they don't know how clever he is . . . he's still hiding in woods, he's still . . .*

But my gut knew; the intense pain in my stomach wasn't letting up—it was a forever kind of pain. *No, no, no, no, no, no. Please, God, please . . .*

As the effects of the sleeping pills someone doled out to me the night before wore off and my brain fog lifted, the day before rushed back to me—the screams of the other parents and the four final words of the doctor that now struck like an axe: *Your son is dead.*

When we left the firehouse, J.T. and I couldn't face returning home. The farmhouse would feel like a tomb without Jesse's boisterous presence, and I didn't know if I'd ever be able to go home again.

My family brought us to my mom's place in Newtown, where J.T. and I held on to each other and cried as the others handled the sudden burst of activity that was already under way by the time we got there—visits from the FBI, questions from police, non-stop calls from family and friends . . . and the media. Newspaper reporters were asking for interviews and photos of Jesse. Someone said an obituary had to be prepared right away and asked if I wanted to write it, but I couldn't. It was all too much, so I swallowed the sleeping pill and collapsed into bed.

But in the morning I knew I was the only one who *could* write Jesse's obituary; I wanted the world to see Jesse through the loving eyes of his mama. I lay in bed in the dark with my stomach still churning, and thought how actually writing my sweet Jesse's name next to the words *Taken from us suddenly on December 14, 2012* would make it official: Jesse was dead. I also thought about how I didn't want to live without him; it would be much, much easier just to die myself. I opened my eyes and whispered, "Oh, Jesse, my Sweet Boy of Joy . . . you can't be gone!"

Suddenly the lamp on the bedside table next to me flickered.

"Jesse?"

The bulb flickered again, in a rapid, steady, staccato rhythm.

Since beginning my spiritual journey years before, I had read about people who believed that blinking lights following the death of a loved one were messages sent from heaven. I hadn't given these claims any particular credence or even thought about them much—until now. As soon as that light blinked, I knew beyond a doubt that it was Jesse reaching out to me.

My stomach pain eased and I felt a comforting warmth wash over me—my boy was letting me know he was still with me. Out loud, I said happily, "Oh, thank you, Jesse! I know you are here!"

Those first five waking minutes on December 15th set the pattern my mornings (and entire days) would follow for months to come. I would awake in blissful ignorance of my loss, experience the sudden gut-wrenching pain of remembering, feel the blinding mental anguish as denial clashed with reality, and then gratefully take a bit of comfort knowing Jesse was trying to communicate with me.

But during those first few months any comfort I found was fleeting. And that first morning it vanished within just a few minutes. When I checked my cell phone for messages, there was a text from Neil informing me that Jesse had been eulogized on the front page of the *New York Post*. I went online, and when the front page of the newspaper appeared on my computer screen, I turned away in horror. The headline screamed, AT LEAST 27 PEOPLE, INCLUDING 20 CHILDREN, SHOT DEAD . . .

It was the first I'd learned of the scope of the

Jesse crashing girls-night-in with (L to R) me, Ashly, Pam, and Jenn. They stayed by my side after his death.

tragedy, the number of innocent lives that had been snuffed out and how many other families had been shattered and were suffering, too. The enormity was too much for me to bear. From that moment forward I blocked out any news about the tragedy—I was living it, I didn't need 24-hour updates. I powered down my phone, put my face in my hands, and sobbed.

What I needed was comfort, not more pain; so thank God for friends and family.

As the day progressed, my closest girlfriends began arriving at my mom's house from all over the country. They stayed for days, and in some cases weeks. They joined a team of loved ones who ensured that I was never alone when my grief was darkest, and that I never woke up without someone next to me during those first weeks.

That evening my dear neighbors Roberta and Chan (who had recommended Beacon Hill Church to me) came over with Pastor Rich and brought along Greg, the youth pastor, to speak with J.T. We prayed together that Jesus would welcome Jesse and all the other little children into his loving arms. Then Pastor Rich told me the next morning's Sunday service would be dedicated to Jesse.

At that service, friends got up and spoke beautiful words about Jesse, and then I got up to talk. I wasn't sure whether or not I would be able to speak, or what I was going to say if I could. But when I stood up that day in front of the congregation, words just came to me. It was the first time I'd spoken publicly about my premonition about Jesse. "I know Jesse is in heaven," I told them, "and he's perfect and he's fine and it's really hard, but I'm okay. I knew that Jesse would be taken from me early."

I explained that ever since he was born, I sensed Jesse would not be with us for long—that God needed him and would call him home early. His light was too bright for this world. I shared Jesse's Prayer with them and the other ways the Lord had moved in my life in recent weeks to prepare both Jesse and me for his passing, including how we started attending services at that very church.

"I know Jesse is still with me. And I no longer fear death, because love never ends."

And death really didn't frighten me anymore—it was *life* that was going to be the challenge.

I felt unwillingly strapped into the front seat of the world's highest roller coaster, and the downs were so fast that it felt like I was going to slam into the earth and die. But the upswings were even worse, because as

I slowly travelled up . . . tick, tick, tick . . . there was no escaping the eventual fall.

One of my first major challenges came that afternoon, when I would come face-to-face with other parents who had lost children in the shooting. We had all been invited to meet with President Obama, who was coming to Sandy Hook to offer his condolences. I slowly realized that my grief would not be a private matter—the world was watching.

The President was scheduled to speak about the tragedy at the local high school, and his remarks would eventually be broadcast around the world. State Trooper Rob Maurice escorted my family to the school—all the parents were assigned a state trooper to protect us and help us navigate through the sea of international media and curious onlookers that had flooded into Sandy Hook.

I clutched J.T.'s hand as Trooper Rob led us (and as many family and friends the secret service had allowed me to bring—about a dozen in total) to a room near the auditorium at Newtown High School, where we waited with other families to have a private moment with the President.

A few minutes later, President Obama came in. I had been brought up in a Republican household, and that had always been my political affiliation. But when he walked into that room and approached my family with such genuine empathy and pain in his eyes, politics no longer mattered.

"Where is the mother?" he asked, as he walked toward us.

President Obama could see Jesse's "bravery"
when I showed him a photo of Jess.

"I'm the mom," I said.

He wrapped his arms around me and gave me a heartfelt hug. We were the last family he came to comfort that day, and he must have been exhausted. But he stayed with us for a while, and before he left he asked me, "Do you have a picture of your son?"

I held up my phone and showed him a picture of Jesse in his soccer uniform.

"I just want you to know," I told the President, "that my son died acting bravely while trying to save the lives of his friends." Police investigators had already given us bits of information they had gathered. They told us that all they knew so far was that Jesse had done something to help some of his classmates get out of the classroom and get to safety. I had known that in my gut back at the firehouse.

President Obama took the phone from my hand and studied Jesse's picture for several minutes before looking up at me and saying, "I can tell from this picture that his bravery did not surprise you at all. I can tell that about him just by looking at this picture."

"Yes sir, you are right about that," I said. "It didn't surprise me at all."

Before the President left us, he shook J.T.'s hand and gave him a hug and made sure to hug my mom, too. And I appreciated the sweet way he shared with me what he saw in Jesse—not like a politician to a victim, but with kindness and honesty, parent to parent.

On our way to the auditorium for the President's speech, the lights in the corridor began flickering wildly above our heads. "Mom, Jesse's here!" said J.T. I squeezed his hand tightly. We had talked about blinking lights as one way loved ones can communicate with us from heaven, and I was happy that we were both picking up on the sign.

After we took our seats and the President began to speak, I closed my eyes and pictured Jesse standing in front of the car the last time I saw him alive, posing next to the message he had just etched in frost for me: *I Love You.*

"I come to offer the love and prayers of a nation," the President said. "I am very mindful that mere words cannot match the depths of your sorrow, nor can they heal your wounded hearts."

I couldn't focus on what he said next because I'd buried my face in J.T.'s shoulder and sobbed for the rest of his speech. Later I would read the transcript of his words in its entirety, and was most moved by these powerful lines: "Can we honestly say that we're doing enough to keep our children—all of them—safe from harm? Can we claim, as a nation, that we're all together there, letting them know that they are loved, and teaching them to love in return? . . . I've been reflecting on this the last few days, and if we're honest with ourselves, the answer is no. We're not doing enough. And we will have to change."

Without either of us knowing it, the President's words planted a seed of healing within my heart. He was right; we weren't doing enough and we did have to change. But, as you will see, it was Jesse who would show me what had to change, and what we needed to do.

CHAPTER
FOUR

Sacred Grieving

The pain I experienced every morning when I woke up—and throughout the day—was so excruciating that a physician suggested I start on antidepressants and antianxiety medication. But I had tried that route in the past when I'd had anxiety attacks in my 20s, and didn't like it. I didn't want to be numbed, especially now, no matter how much I hurt. I wanted to be fully aware of this experience and fully present for J.T. when he needed me most. I took sleeping pills because I knew I wouldn't function without sleep and I had to protect my energy—but that was the only drug I allowed myself.

So instead of medication, each morning I forced myself to get out of bed and dragged myself to the kitchen, hoping that the familiar act of making a cup of tea would restore a sense of routine. My usual morning routine had died with Jesse, and I needed to establish a new one to occupy my thoughts so that my imagination wouldn't conjure up horrific images of what had happened in that classroom, images that started to flash through my mind moments after I awoke. I made the tea, but I couldn't drink it. I could barely keep any food down. Oddly, the only thing that seemed to settle my stomach was the champagne that I'd sip anytime our family toasted to Jesse's life in the evenings.

Even though I was trying to get sleep and preserve my energy, I was wiped out and just wanted to sink into my mother's couch and not move or talk to any-body. Which is why, I suppose, I'd been avoiding Dr. Laura's calls.

Dr. Laura Asher, like Trooper Rob Maurice, had been assigned to me by the state in the unenviable role of personal grief counselor. But I didn't want counsel-ing, I wanted to be left alone—the last thing I needed was a stranger urging me to open up and share my feelings. She'd been leaving me voice mails and texts, but I hadn't returned any of them.

But God bless her, Dr. Laura would not give up, and eventually she tracked me down at my mother's house. She arrived on our doorstep accompanied by a state trooper escort of her own. At the very same time a social worker also showed up unexpectedly to help me. I told the social worker to wait on the couch next to me as I braced myself for a torturous hour of therapy, but my first grief counseling session with Dr. Laura turned out to be nothing like what I had expected, and it helped me in ways I could not have imagined.

Dr. Laura immediately put me at ease with her warm, gentle demeanor. I was drawn to the deep spiri-tual energy that radiated from this beautiful woman who, I later learned, was a family physician, a disaster-relief counselor, a practitioner of holistic medicine, a massage therapist, a philosopher, a teacher, *and* an interfaith minister.

"I have been praying for you," Dr. Laura said softly, and then she asked me to remove my shoes and socks.

"And while I prayed, I felt the strong presence of Jesus's mother around me," she continued. Dr. Laura then told me that she'd had a powerful dream early that morning of the Blessed Mother, who spoke to her about me.

"Mother Mary wants you to know she is grieving for Jesse, too—she is weeping with you and she is weeping for you."

It seemed an odd thing for a state-appointed doctor to say, but Laura was so genuine and kind that I believed her immediately and completely. And then she said something astonishing.

"Mother Mary sent me here to wash your feet."

Dr. Laura asked the social worker and my mother to prepare a large bowl of warm water, lavender, and olive oil and place it on the floor in front of me. Then she knelt by it and slowly washed my feet in the warm, soothing liquid. As she massaged the oil into my skin, she explained the ritual of foot washing and told me that it had been performed for thousands of years as an act of cleansing, a ceremony that helped souls suffering through extreme emotional turmoil to find peace and to heal.

"Grieving is a sacred act; we must respect it and treat it as such," Dr. Laura said.

At one point during the ceremony, Dr. Laura asked my mother to bring me something special and beautiful of hers. My mother went upstairs and came back down and handed me a polished, triple strand "turk boys" necklace with an engraving that said, "When it seems like it is the darkest of days and there is no light, remember this beautiful sky-blue stone came from a black beginning."

I closed my eyes and thought about the first words Dr. Laura had spoken to me—Mother Mary was weeping for me and with me. I remembered having read in the Bible that when Mary carried the infant Jesus into the temple to be blessed, she received a prophecy that her newborn son would be taken from her early and whatever agony he suffered, she would suffer just as sharply. Then I thought of Mother Mary kneeling beneath the cross, cradling the body of her innocent boy, a boy who had sacrificed his own life to save others. A sudden love for Mary came over me, as well as a deep sense of kinship with her that continues to this day.

When I opened my eyes, I saw that Dr. Laura had removed her scarf from her shoulders and was using it to dry my feet, while the social worker read aloud comforting verses from the Bible, which had been chosen by Dr. Laura. Some verses described Jesus having *his* feet washed and others recounted stories of Jesus washing the feet of his followers.

By this time at least a dozen friends and family had drifted into the room, all deeply moved by the powerful, loving ritual. Dr. Laura's state trooper sat off to the side on my mother's piano bench with tears streaming down his cheeks. Toward the end of the ceremony, the social worker knelt beside me, placed her hand on my knee, and confided that she, too, had experienced the heartbreak of losing a child.

"Years ago I lost my son . . . my only son," she began. I was suddenly riveted. The mention of losing a child made me focus with laserlike intensity. I leaned down to listen to her, assuming her suffering had provided her with insight into enduring the grieving process. She seemed compelled and eager to pass the benefit of her experience along to me, and I needed desperately to hear her words of wisdom and encouragement. But her words stung me like a slap in the face.

"Scarlett, I have to tell you that it doesn't get any better—it will never get better. You will always feel this pain."

I could not believe what this woman had just said to me. How dare she set negative limits on my healing process? The woman was about to continue to speak when I put my hand up as if to stay *stop right there*.

"I don't want to hear this!" I said to her. "This is not for me! How can you tell me it's not going to get better? Your path is not my path. I am going to go on my own journey . . . *I am going to have my own journey!*"

Dr. Laura moved in and put her hand on my shoulder, nodding reassuringly, telling me that, yes, this journey most definitely *was* my own and would be as unique to me as my own DNA. It had only just begun, she added, and I would be surprised at where it would lead me.

I smiled; Dr. Laura was perfect for me.

That moment was one of several turning points for me. By claiming my grieving process as my own I was taking a major step toward healing. Maybe the social worker was correct and I *would* always carry the pain of Jesse's death with me. But she was wrong to tell me it would never get any better, dooming me to a life of despair. If I had believed her, believed that it wouldn't get any better, I might have ended it all right then.

Actually, I should have thanked that woman for what she said, because she taught me an important lesson about the sacred act of grieving—and of living. She taught me that even though I couldn't choose what had happened to me or Jesse, I could choose the way I reacted.

As I stood barefoot in my mother's living room, I silently vowed never to allow anyone other than me to determine the course my grief would take—or the course of my life. It was true that my pain was immense, but it was also true that I had hope. I knew that Jesse's spirit was with me, and I knew that love never ends.

That "knowing" is what pulled me through the next difficult days as I said good-bye to my boy.

PART II | SIGNS

CHAPTER FIVE | Hearts to Heaven

Jesse's wake was a welcome sorrow. I wanted to see him, but not in a casket. I'd been yearning to hold his body close to me since the moment I knew he was gone, but the ensuing police investigation and autopsy prevented that from happening. At our private family wake I would be alone with my son for the first time since his death, and for one last time. The finality of that was too much to contemplate, and I said a prayer for strength—and for Jesse to send me a sign that he was okay and that his spirit was still close to me.

My prayer was answered when my sister-in-law Becky arrived at the house a little later that morning. Becky is married to my brother Jordan and is the mother of Jesse's two-year-old cousin, Christian. I'd given little Christian a toy train that I'd bought for Jesse as an early Christmas present, a train that Jesse had loved and that I knew he would have wanted his cousin to have.

"I don't know how to begin to tell you this . . ." Becky said, her eyes red and swollen from crying. "But . . . Jesse was in our house," she blurted out. Then she told me what happened.

Christian playing with Jesse's train

"Ever since you gave Christian that train, he's been obsessed with it. Really early this morning, Jordan and the baby and I were in bed, and I could hear Christian out in the hall playing with the train. Our door is closed but I can hear him . . . and he barely talks, but I can hear him *talking* . . . having a conversation! I listen very closely and I hear him say, 'What you talking about?' Then he pauses, like he's listening to someone answer him, and he asks, 'Oh . . . this *your* cool train?' And then another pause, and he says, 'Yeah, I could try it in the bathtub!' I looked at Jordan and he looked at me, and we knew— *Christian is talking to Jesse!*"

Becky and Jordan were certain Jesse had just talked to their son; and I was certain Jesse had just talked to me through his little cousin—and he told me what I needed to hear: he was okay and he was with me.

The night before the wake, I had another sign. I had gotten up in the middle of the night to use the bathroom, and when I got back to my bed, one of Jesse's little army men was lying in the middle of my pillow! I did what would become my routine over the next few months: each time I got what I was sure was a sign, I looked heavenward, and said, "Thank you, Jesse!"

I didn't know how else to explain these little happenings except to conclude that it was Jesse speaking to me. I wasn't imagining them, and others in the family were experiencing lights flashing even when they had turned the light switch off. I was sure they were signs and that Jesse was trying to give me the strength I'd need when I'd see him in his casket.

I remember walking into the funeral home, my heart pounding in my chest. I was afraid, but at the same time I couldn't wait to see Jesse again. I approached the little white casket tentatively . . . and saw my precious boy. They had done a good job of concealing his wounds, but no matter how talented the makeup people were, they couldn't give Jesse that sweet smile that had lit up my life. His sweet, angelic face looked like Jesse on the outside, but I knew his spirit was no longer there on the inside.

I took his hands in mine and studied his fingers, and saw that he still had dirt under his fingernails from playing at the farm. I tried to warm his little hands with my own. I sat next to him for the next three hours, holding his hand, taking in every detail of his little body before he was gone forever. When it was time to leave, I didn't move.

"No. I'm going to sleep next to him here, on the floor, next to his casket. I'll sleep on a blanket," I told my mother, matter-of-factly. She went to ask the funeral parlor owner if this was possible and returned saying they would not allow it.

"Is he going to drag me away?" I asked my mother. "Are the police going to come and drag me away?"

We stayed an extra hour past closing time, and my family gently but firmly guided me away from the casket and drove me home. The need for sleep was what finally persuaded me to leave; I knew I'd need rest and strength for what was to come.

The next day was Jesse's funeral, but before that, my family had arranged a public wake. I was stunned by the turnout; thousands of people came. Trooper Rob, who had quickly become like family, escorted us through the crowd and into the funeral home, which was packed. Many of the attendees were people I knew, but most were strangers. Some members of a Native American tribe had driven all the way from South Dakota to pay tribute to Jesse. I didn't see them because, as Dr. Laura described it, even though I was trying to be as present as possible, I was still in my "grief bubble." But they stood out among the supporters, so Dr. Laura spotted them, and as soon as she did, she made a beeline to the chief to find out what had brought them such a distance.

"We knew a great spirit had passed from the world," the chief told her, "and we felt the spirit ascend to the top of a mountain—that's how elevated it is. And then we felt the spirit ascend again to the top of that mountain's mountain. So we came to honor such a great spirit and pay our respects."

After hundreds of people had passed by Jesse's coffin, the viewing area was cleared so family and close friends could have a last, private moment.

Once again I stood at the casket and once again I held on to Jesse's hands. Each member of the family left a gift for Jesse to take on his journey. J.T. left his little brother a ceramic bluebird that Kristy had made for each of the family members in honor of Jesse's love of birds. I pinned a little red baby bird that I'd been wearing next to a bigger red mama bird on his shirt. The baby bird had a banner at the bottom that said "Branch of Jesse." I also left him with plenty of ducks and toy soldiers to play with, which I had scooped up from the bathroom tub when I'd gone to the farm to pick out his burial clothes. Then I took a deep breath and slowly slid his army helmet in beside him—just in case he wanted to go on patrol in front of the pearly gates in heaven. The last thing I did for Jesse was to wrap him up in the warm woolen Indian blanket I'd worn draped around me the previous night so that it smelled like "mama," and had my essence. I tucked him in for the long night ahead and kissed my Sweet Boy of Joy good-bye . . . until we meet again.

A cortege of 40 police officers marched to Jesse's casket two at a time and saluted him.

And then they closed the lid.

My brothers and stepfather Bob carried Jesse's casket to the hearse, and we left for the church.

The procession was lit up and it felt a mile long. We were led by police cars and surrounded by motorcycles.

Even though the temperature outside was freezing, hundreds of people pulled to the side of the road as we were passing, got out of their cars, removed their hats, and put their hands to their hearts; some also saluted. Through the car window, I could see some people get down on their knees on the pavement and bow their heads. I smiled with the rest of the family and we all agreed: Jesse was loving this.

At the church service Jesse was eulogized with funny anecdotes about his boisterous nature, many kind acts, and sweetness of personality. My brother Trent mentioned that the one rule Jesse always followed was his own rule to "have a lot of fun." J.T. remembered that even when he and Jesse fought like brothers do, they still loved each other like brothers do. More than anything, Jesse was remembered for the passion with which he loved life and loved others—and the way he urged those around him to do the same.

Then it was my turn.

"People have been asking me since the tragedy what they can do to help," I told the packed church. "If you really want to do something to help, then do something that will help all of us by turning an angry thought into a loving one. This whole tragedy began with an angry thought, and that thought could have been changed to a loving one. If it had been, none of us would be here today to bury a child we all loved so much. So if you want to do something to help, then do what Jesse would have wanted you to do to honor his memory—take just one angry thought you have each day and turn it into a loving one . . . and with one loving thought at a time, we will change the world and make it a better, safer place for our children and our

Police officers saluted as we made our way to the cemetery.

children's children. If you want to help, then please choose love."

Once again, we were escorted to the cemetery in the midst of a police motorcade, with lights flashing and sirens wailing. A squadron of motorcycle officers flanked the motorcade, and those who rode ahead of us dismounted at every intersection to stop traffic, and they stood at attention to salute Jesse as the hearse passed by. When we arrived at the cemetery gates, we were greeted by a column of mounted police who saluted Jesse from atop their huge, magnificent horses—the kind of giant animals Jesse loved and had no fear of riding.

When his casket arrived at the grave site, I felt Jesse's spirit all around us, especially as he was lowered to rest to the ethereal voice of Celine Dion singing the beautiful lyrics of "Fly," which expressed exactly what I wanted to say at that moment.

While the music played, my young friend Kelly moved among us handing out 20 brightly colored balloons—one for each lost child. I took J.T.'s hand in mine, and we all walked together to a clearing and set the balloons free, watching them rise upward on the wind as they slowly drifted toward town. A moment later, someone capturing the scene with a video camera shouted "Oh my God, look . . . the balloons! They've formed a heart!"

It seemed miraculous, but sure enough, the balloons had come together and were floating directly above Sandy Hook Elementary in the shape of a heart. For several minutes the heart hovered above the school where just six days before the souls of 20 innocent children had left the world.

It was an amazing sight, and if I hadn't seen it with my own eyes, I don't know if I would have believed it.

Then the wind picked up, and the beautiful heart floated up to heaven.

CHAPTER SIX | Energies AND Messages

To me, the balloons rising to heaven as a perfectly shaped heart after Jesse's funeral was a divinely orchestrated event. Once again, I'm sure many would write it off as a coincidence, an optical illusion, a flight of fancy, or just the wishful thinking of a grieving mother. But it wasn't; others saw it, too. And not only that—so many people had begun telling me about the supernatural experiences they'd had in the past few days that I was certain something special was happening. I could feel Jesse's energy swirling around my family and friends, gaining in both power and momentum.

My friend Ashly and her husband, Rick, told us they were waking up suddenly at exactly 3 A.M. every morning with overwhelming thoughts of Jesse.

And just the night before, my brother Trent had jolted awake at exactly 3 A.M. with a powerful sensation that someone's hand was pressing down on his chest. He looked next to his bed and saw what he describes as a Native American angel standing in his room. The angel's arms were feathered like wings, and he had a halo above his head that illuminated the zigzag pattern of black-and-white war paint streaked across his face.

"I wasn't afraid; I was just startled," he told me over the phone. "His face kept alternating between deep sorrow and ferocious anger. I thought he was some kind of warrior angel upset by what had happened to Jesse."

The only other mystical experience Trent ever had was years ago when he had a dream of our grandmother placing J.T.'s hand into his own. It didn't mean anything to us at the time, but in hindsight, with Trent being J.T.'s godfather, I believe it was our grandmother telling him to watch over J.T. because he was going to be needing Trent's help.

Using the details Trent gave me, I went online to search for what his vision could mean. When I hit the Enter button, a glorious image of a shaman angel appeared on my computer screen. During my spiritual studies, I'd learned that shamans existed in most aboriginal cultures and acted as healers and mediums who'd communicate with the spirit world. In the spirit world, the role of a shaman angel is to guard and protect the members of the tribe. *Now that's Jesse's kind of angel*, I thought.

Supernatural events were happening back home on the farm, too. A couple of months earlier, our dear friends—Jesse's longtime babysitter Marissa and her mom, Susan—had temporarily moved in with us and had become like family. They were still living at the farm while J.T. and I were at my mom's house.

Ready for battle: Jesse and his Army men take a bath.

After the funeral Susan called to ask when J.T. and I were planning to come back home. I told her I didn't think I could ever live at the farm again without Jesse—the house would feel too empty without him.

"Scarlett, you must . . . you *must* come back. Jesse is still here."

"What do you mean?"

Susan told me that she and Marissa had both heard Jesse laughing and running—even whistling—all over the house. One night when Susan entered the bathroom, she saw a shadowy figure in the tub where Jesse used to play with his ducks and soldiers during his long baths. Neither Susan nor Marissa were frightened by what they had seen and heard. They were excited and happy because they knew "beyond any doubt" that it was Jesse's spirit.

"Scarlett, you have to come back here," Marissa said. "Jesse's waiting for you."

.   .   .

Even at Jesse's grave, which I visited at least once a day, his energy was drawing people together through supernatural occurrences. During one of my morning visits, I found two middle-aged women standing at the head of Jesse's grave when I arrived. They were casually dressed in blue jeans and T-shirts, suburban mom types. They were strangers to me, but with so many people visiting the graves of the children who had been killed, I thought nothing of it, except that I was happy Jesse had company.

When I introduced myself as Jesse's mother, the women looked at each other with excitement and told me that they were psychics and had driven for several hours to deliver a message to me from Jesse. I'd never spoken to a psychic before, but I had been asking Jesse every day to send me messages, so I wasn't about to dismiss people who'd shown up at his grave telling me Jesse had sent them to do just that.

"Well, first of all, as I'm sure you know, he's okay—he just wanted me to reassure you of that," one of them said. "And he also wants you to know that he's very proud about what he did at the school."

I nodded and smiled, thinking about what we'd heard from the police. I was proud of him, too.

We talked a bit more, and it was all very surreal. If someone had told me two weeks earlier that I'd be standing beside my son's grave listening to a couple of psychic soccer moms passing along messages from Jesse from the afterlife, I would have laughed. But these women were speaking a language I was starting to understand—the language of spirit, energy, and supernatural messages.

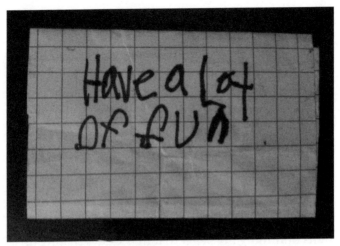

A special message for his brother, J.T.

Jesse was regularly sending me small signs from the other side, messages I desperately wanted to hear. And, as it would turn out, they were also his way of preparing me for bigger and very important messages still to come.

After leaving the cemetery, I picked up J.T. and drove to the farm to collect some clean clothes for a trip he and I were taking to Orlando the day after Christmas—it was J.T.'s big Christmas gift this year. I thought it would be good for us to get away for a few days in the sun to reconnect as our new family unit of two. After packing a suitcase in his room, J.T. came into the kitchen with a big grin.

"Mom, you know how everybody is getting messages from Jesse? Well I just got one!" he said, showing me a small, handwritten note. "This was in my room under my desk," he said. "I have no idea how it got there, but it's from Jesse!" J.T. was certain Jesse wrote it a day or two before he was killed, because he'd never seen it before. The note was in Jesse's unmistakable and adorably childlike printing: *Have a Lot of fun.*

It was pure Jesse—short, sweet, simple, and impossible to ignore. And it was the same message my brother Trent had used in his eulogy a week or so earlier to describe Jesse's philosophy of life. And now here it was again: *Have a Lot of fun.* This time it was a message from Jesse telling his brother not to be too sad and to enjoy his life.

The following day I was presented with yet another sign confirming my belief that in the days leading up to the shooting, Jesse was subconsciously aware of what was to happen. Trooper Rob came to my mom's with a box of Jesse's personal belongings from the school. It contained all of his assignments and artwork, most of them dated and stacked in chronological order starting with the oldest schoolwork—from November—on top.

My mom, my sisters-in-law, and I sat on the living room floor and sorted through the material. At the very bottom of the box, beneath work dated just a few days before the shooting, was a pencil drawing by Jesse that made me shudder. It was a picture of two figures—one a small, smiling boy with angel wings . . . the other a much taller and menacing figure whose face Jesse had obliterated by scribbling over it repeatedly. It was obvious to both my mother and me what the picture represented; it was my brave Jesse, soon to be in heaven, confronting the gunman. And it further confirmed to me that Jesse had a spiritual knowing of what was to be, and that he himself was part of God's bigger master plan.

The angel and a bad man: Jesse drew this days before the shooting

On Christmas morning I woke suddenly at 3 A.M. A minute later the laptop on the desk booted up, and the printer turned on with a noisy beep-beep-beep! *And a very Merry Christmas to you, too, Jesse.*

That afternoon, I left a message for Jesse at the place where he died.

Trooper Rob escorted me and some other members of my family to Sandy Hook Elementary. The families of the victims had been invited to visit the school grounds. It was the first time anyone other than investigators had been near the school since the shooting. We weren't allowed to go inside but could walk around freely outside the building. At first I'd hesitated to accept the invitation, fearing the experience would prove too painful. But something Dr. Laura said changed my mind: "In Native American tradition, the place where a warrior is slain is considered sacred ground."

That made me think about the Native Americans at Jesse's wake and of Trent's vision of the shaman angel. I decided that if the school really was sacred ground, I owed it to Jesse to honor him there.

We stood in front of the school, and I read a Native American prayer. Miss Soto's family had come earlier in the day and written sweet messages to her on the plywood that was boarding up the front doors. I took a marker from my purse and left a message for Jesse.

Our angel and guardian angel . . . we are so proud of you, we love you, (heart) with Jesse + Mama, TLF, TLA (true love forever, true love always).

And then I wrote "J.T." and surrounded it with little hearts, and I thought of the balloons that formed a heart above this very spot before ascending to heaven. Dr. Laura was so right—this was indeed sacred ground. I looked down at the ground and saw shattered glass everywhere.

"Everybody . . . pick up a piece of glass," I said to the group, and everybody did, even Trooper Rob. I held up my own shard and said, "These bits of glass signify Jesse's bravery. Carry one with you as a reminder that even when we are most frightened, when we don't know if we can find courage, that we can be brave like Jesse."

I slipped the glass into my purse; I would need a lot of courage in the coming days and years.

. . .

"Most important, brothers love" J.T. wrote in his of eulogy of little brother Jesse.

That night I went to J.T.'s room and gave him an ornament Jesse had bought for him as a Christmas present just before he died. It was a ball with a little heart, and in the middle of the heart was the word *Brothers*. Jesse had purchased an identical one for me, but with the word *Mother*. J.T. held it and cried, falling asleep clutching the ornament to his chest.

Both of us had now received gifts and messages from Jesse to help us be strong and have hope. I looked at J.T. sleeping peacefully—we were a duo again, like we'd been before Jesse arrived, when I used to tow him around in his red wagon. But this time around, we had a tougher road to travel; no doubt about that.

But I was determined we'd make the road our own, and our journey together would be filled with love and healing.

I leaned over and kissed J.T.'s cheek. How could I not?

CHAPTER
SEVEN

Jesse
IN THE SKY
WITH Jesus

My trip to Orlando with J.T. was intended as a "healing vacation" for the two of us, and it turned out to be just that—and in some very unexpected ways.

Even though I was determined to build a new life for J.T. and myself, I was so consumed with grief that any future I imagined was one filled with suffering, and any choice I considered was clouded by pain. Orlando changed that. I don't know if it was the hand of God or a kick in the rear end from Jesse, but in the time it took me to fly out of the East Coast winter and step into the Florida sunshine, the clouds had started to lift. And by the time our trip was over, my vision had cleared and I had hope for the future.

The shift in my thinking began when J.T. and I were weaving through the bustling departures concourse at JFK. It seemed as though every person streaming past me—either on their way to an adventure or just coming from one—looked utterly miserable. Everywhere I glanced I saw long-suffering, world-weary faces. Seeing so much unhappiness in one place—a place that *wasn't* Sandy Hook—was surreal and unnerving. But we were in a rush to get to the boarding gate, so by the time J.T. and I had reached the security check I'd pushed the uncomfortable feeling aside.

During the flight J.T. watched a movie, which I might have done, too, if the TV screen in front of me hadn't kept flickering off and on every time I picked a channel. J.T. tried to help, but the flickering happened every time he touched the screen as well. We smiled and nodded to each other. *Jesse.* And it wasn't just the flickering screen—when I tried to listen to music from the in-flight selection, the song I chose skipped to a different one that was either a favorite of Jesse's or had lyrics that reminded me of him or how I was feeling. Finally I just settled back into my seat and relaxed, happy to know that Jesse had decided to come along with his mom and big brother on our "healing trip."

As J.T. and I waited at the Orlando luggage carousel for our bags to arrive, the uncomfortable feeling I'd brushed aside at JFK returned. Again, it was the faces in the crowd that unsettled me. They looked haunted, like the walking dead. All I was able to see was their despair and pain—no joy, no love and forgiveness, no spark of God. My stomach tightened as I wondered if that's what they saw when they looked at me. *Oh Lord, am I just like them? No! I do not want to be like these people. I am not dead yet! I refuse to exist just to carry my pain from one day to the next. I have a life to live, and I want to be happy for J.T. and for myself. Sometimes I struggle and feel like dying, but I am going to choose life . . . I am going to choose love. I won't be a prisoner of my pain; I will find a way to deal with it, and I will make my life count for something.*

I wanted to live a full life, and I wanted to do

something to prevent others from going through the suffering that I and the other Sandy Hook parents were experiencing. I just had to find a way.

I checked my e-mail as J.T and I waited for the rental car and found a message from one of the psychics I'd met at Jesse's grave site. Before we'd boarded, I'd e-mailed her a list of the amazing messages Jesse had been sending me. My eyes welled up as I read her response: "Maybe Jesse is lingering here and not moving onward because he wants to make sure you and J.T. are okay. Spirits do that sometimes."

Her words were a blow. I didn't want to break down in front of J.T., so I excused myself to go to the restroom, where I locked myself into a stall and began bawling uncontrollably. Was the psychic telling me that Jesse could not move upward to heaven because of my grief? Was I being selfish keeping him here, holding him down, asking him to send me messages when he could be in the loving arms of Jesus and playing in heaven?

If that were true, I knew what I had to do next, no matter how much I wanted him near me—I had to let Jesse go. I wailed hysterically at that thought, and then I pushed through my tears and said out loud, "Jesse, you've been so precious sending such sweet messages to let us know you're okay and to comfort us. But you have to listen to your mama now. We are going to be okay, J.T. and I. You can go to Jesus now, do you hear me, sweet boy? Go to Jesus; we will be okay. Always know how much I love you."

I'm not sure how long I cried in that stall, but somehow I managed to dry my tears and compose myself before returning to J.T. and signing for our rental car. I gave J.T. a hug and said, "Okay, J.T. It's you and me. Let's go *have a lot of fun."*

We'd only been on the road for a few minutes when I looked up and saw it—a message written across the blue Florida sky in white, puffy letters a hundred feet high and more than a mile wide that read: JESSE & JESUS. TOGETHER FOREVER.

Was I imagining this? Could this be real? I looked over at J.T. There was no way I was going to say it first. He was looking up, too, and then he turned to me. "Mom! Jesse's with Jesus!"

My heart was racing. This time it wasn't a flickering light; this time it was spelled out in giant letters that could be seen by hundreds of people for 20 miles in any direction and was hanging over the city of Orlando like a billboard in the sky. There was no mistaking the message and no mistaking that it was for us—the name "Jesse" was even written with a backward "J" just as Jesse used to do it. Jesse was letting me know that he had heard me and was telling me to be happy because he *was* in the arms of Jesus. I'm not sure if I'd misunderstood what the psychic was trying to say in her e-mail, but if she had meant that Jesse was not in heaven yet, she was wrong. He wasn't stuck in some earthbound plane; he was speaking to us from heaven. What a miraculous affirmation! I pulled over to the side of the road, and J.T. and I sat in silence and just looked up at the sky. We were in awe. It was the most incredible thing to ever happen to us.

Jesse! Thank you, thank you, thank you! And thank you, Jesus . . . please take good care of my sweet boy!

Jesse writes to us in the Orlando sky.

A small plane was flying just below the message leaving a trail of white smoke in its wake. It was a sky-writing plane, but who the pilot was or why he or she was filling the sky with this message from my son was a mystery. There were only a handful of people who even knew we were in Florida, and *nobody* knew our whereabouts at that precise moment. Not only had bad weather forced us to change departure airports at the last minute, but our flight had been switched three times.

We quickly snapped some photos of the message because it started to disappear fast, then the plane circled back and began writing a second message. As the letters and symbols took shape, I surprised myself by laughing. Jesse was such a sweet, clever boy to have found a way to slip a little joy into his mama's broken heart. J.T. was looking up and smiling as well.

The second message was this: $\text{U} + \text{GOD} = \text{☺}$.

Math was one of Jesse's best subjects, and he'd just sent his mother and brother a brilliant equation on how to live a happy life—by staying close to God. And that is exactly what I planned to do, and I would do everything in my power to help J.T. do the same. We got back into the car and prayed together, thankful for Jesse's message in the sky. We prayed for continued strength and courage, and we prayed for all the children and adults who'd lost their lives that day with Jesse. It was true; love never ends. Could anyone ask for a clearer message from heaven?

I didn't think so, but it seemed Jesse wanted to make doubly sure that we had no doubt it was him sending us smoke signals from beyond, as I discovered when my brother Trent phoned me at our hotel later that night. Trent was tucking his three-year-old son, Hayden (another of Jesse's little cousins), into bed, and he asked him, "Why don't we say good night to your cousin Jesse?" To which Hayden replied, "Jesse? Oh, Jesse is flying! He's flying in the sky!"

Despite the miraculous signs I'd just received, I was still only human, and waking up in Florida was just as agonizing as waking up in Connecticut. But I quickly remembered the hope-filled messages Jesse sent and felt grateful. I got out of bed and woke up J.T., and told him we had to do as Jesse had instructed and have a lot of fun. And we did. It was great to be together in the warm sunshine and be physically active again. We played volleyball in the pool, enjoyed a few sets of tennis, went snorkeling among the colorful tropical fish,

J.T. with a "golphin" during our healing trip to Orlando.

and even swam with a dolphin named Rose, the same name as the mama horse in *Rose's Foal*—Jesse would have loved that. Both J.T. and I smiled, remembering how crazy Jesse was about dolphins, which he called "golphins."

Our most exciting outing was a helicopter ride that distracted us from reality for 12 blissful minutes. But the reality of Sandy Hook was inescapable, even in a tropical paradise. One evening while we were relaxing in the hot tub beside the Tacky Tiki Club bar, we were joined by Canadian vacationers who asked us where we were from.

"Oh my gosh, you're from Newtown?" one woman asked. "Isn't that where . . . ?"

I quickly raised my hand up like a crossing guard warding off a reckless driver. The woman got the hint, thankfully, and J.T. and I left the hot tub without a word, but on the way up to our room he said, "Mom, from now on, if someone asks us where we are from, let's just say New York."

For the most part our Florida trip was good. But one of the lessons my grief was teaching me was that healing takes time, and its path is unpredictable. I struggled to keep my mind from going to dark places—blaming myself, regretting things I had done or didn't do, and imagining the details of what Jesse went through in his last moments. If it was difficult for me, a grown woman who had read extensively about the power of the mind and positive thinking, God only knew how difficult it was for J.T. And to make matters worse, he had the usual angst, confusion, and emotional challenges of adolescence to deal with on top of his grief.

Our last day in Orlando was on New Year's Eve, and J.T. seemed especially sad, but he wouldn't talk about it with me. I had a phone therapy session set up with Dr. Laura, so I included him on the call—she always encouraged and comforted me, and I hoped she'd have the same effect on J.T.

But when Dr. Laura asked J.T. how he was feeling, he stormed out of the room. I sat there with the phone in my hand realizing that our "healing trip" was just the first step of a long journey, and that both J.T. and I, understandably, were still avoiding our pain. And if I was going to be a good mom to him, and if I was going to live up to the promise I'd made to myself in the airport to not let pain rule my life, I would have to confront it directly. So on New Year's Day, after we'd returned from Florida, J.T. and I moved back to the farm—it was time to go home.

·   ·   ·

One of the reasons I'd been afraid to go home earlier was because I was worried that if I saw Jesse's things all day every day it would be too emotional for me. I imagined his boots lined up at the door, his toothbrush where he left it by the sink, his pj's crumpled where he last dropped them on the bedroom floor. I was glad he was in heaven, but I didn't think I could handle the daily reminders around the farm that he wasn't with *me*. Pam and Ashly came home with us that first night, and in the living room, I got down on my knees, swept my hand under the coffee table, and pulled out two of Jesse's army men.

"See?" I said, tears in my eyes. "This is my greatest fear! That Jesse's things will just make me sad!"

"No!" Pam got up and took the two army men from my hand. She held them up and reminded me about how hard Jesse had been working to send me signs over the last two weeks.

"These are not here to make you sad; these are gifts! Jesse is leaving them for you, don't you see that?"

She was so right. Her words helped me completely change my perception about it, and from that moment on, I chose to embrace each little gift Jesse "sent" me with happiness and gratitude.

Ashly heated frankincense, myrrh, and amber in a roasting shovel over a bed of burning coals in the fireplace, explaining that these three sacred resins have been used in spiritual, religious, and festive ceremonies for thousands of years. They symbolize the joy or sacredness of an event or place, and they also attract positive energy.

We carried the fragrant mixture into the center of Jesse's room and spoke to him out loud, saying, "We love you, Jesse!" as the soothing fragrance wafted to the ceiling.

What happened next took my breath away. My head began tingling, and I sensed something brushing past my cheek. We all felt it; Jesse's happy, positive spirit breezed into the room and swirled around us for several minutes, then rose upward—a quick, reassuring hello from heaven.

The next morning I got up early and was happy to know that the house was filled with people I love. It really did feel like a new beginning. J.T. was in a great mood after receiving a backpack, T-shirt, and other paraphernalia emblazoned with the name of his favorite TV show, *The Office*, in the mail. The executive producer at NBC had been tipped off that J.T. loved the show and sent the care package to cheer him up. It was wonderful to see J.T. smiling. And our difficult phone session with Dr. Laura had actually gotten us talking, and J.T. had agreed to start seeing his own grief counselor.

I was glad to be back at home. I sat in my kitchen and quietly reflected upon how I could best keep the promise I'd made to myself on our trip to make the rest of my life count for something. I felt a need to help turn this tragedy into something positive for the world. To give back all the incredible generosity of spirit that had been shown to me in my darkest hours. I couldn't imagine going back to any semblance of my previous life— that was gone. I thought about a beautiful letter I had received from a father who had lost his young son from an illness years earlier. He wrote: "I've spent the last 15 years asking myself why—why me, why my son, why

Three words on our kitchen chalkboard that gave me a mission

now, why not someone else? Now I know why. It was so that I could write this letter of comfort to you."

How could I, too, move forward and be of service to others? How could I use my experience to help others in pain and help prevent a tragedy like this from happening again? I had no idea.

But Jesse did.

At that very moment, I glanced over at the chalkboard we had set up years ago in the kitchen to leave little messages for each other, and that is exactly what I saw there now—a new message for me from Jesse that he must have written just before he died.

The message, its letters printed out in Jesse's messy, mixed-up style, had only three little words, but they were big enough to change the world.

"Norurting helin love."

Nurturing, healing love.

PART III | HEALING

Nurturing a Foundation

Seeing a message written across the sky proclaiming "Jesse & Jesus" ten minutes after telling Jesse to *go* to Jesus wasn't a fluke—it happened for a reason.

Jesse's "nurturing healing love" message on the kitchen chalkboard wasn't a coincidence either—he wrote it for a reason.

The message in the sky gave me the comfort, hope, and faith I needed to carry on; the message on the chalkboard gave me a mission.

The structure of the mission would come to me over time and with the help, wisdom, and guidance of others. But the objective of the mission was clear from the start: encouraging people to choose love—finding and sharing ways to nurture, heal, and love one another so that our anger won't reach the point where we want to hurt ourselves or others.

When I thought about it later, I realized that I had actually started my mission on the day of Jesse's funeral.

When I was trying to figure out what I could possibly say to honor Jesse's memory in my eulogy, I remembered one of Mother Teresa's favorite poems, "Anyway," which she had tacked up on the wall of her children's home in Calcutta. It basically says that if someone is mean or unkind to you, love them anyway. The poem, written by Kent M. Keith, seemed to capture Jesse's spirit and the way he lived his life. I read the beautifully inspiring words at the funeral and then asked everyone who had come to the church service to join me in honoring Jesse by consciously changing an angry thought to a loving one—to always choose love. Two days after the funeral, a 66-year-old doctor who was an old and dear friend of my father called Dad and told him how deeply affected he'd been by what I'd said.

"David, I've spent my entire life being angry," he confessed. "It never even occurred to me I had any other choice. But now I know I do, and my life has completely changed." The doctor told Dad that he'd already printed out signs reading "Choose Love" and posted them all over his office.

"I'm telling my staff, my patients, and everyone else I meet to choose love because it is something we can all do; it is a *choice*."

After Dad told me about the immediate and profound effect those words had on his friend, I thought about the potential power of that message. How many patients, I wondered, left this doctor's office inspired to live more loving lives from that moment on, and then went out into the world and inspired others to do the same, setting off a sort of nurturing-healing-love domino effect?

. . .

Reading one of thousands of "love letters" from around the world

The kind of nurturing-healing-love synergy I envisioned was already happening in our town.

It started with handfuls of letters and cards simply addressed to "The People of Sandy Hook" that began trickling in the day after the tragedy. Within a couple of weeks, the U.S. Postal Service had to set up a special sorting station and warehouse to deal with the tons (literally—*tons*) of letters pouring into Newtown from all over the world—from people of all ages, cultures, religions, and walks of life. To date, we've received more than 500,000 letters, posters, cards, and drawings—not to mention the sculptures, toys, teddy bears, and countless other gifts that continue to arrive every day.

At our town hall, thousands of the letters and cards were put on display at an ever-evolving memorial. The first time I went to see it, I was awestruck by the enormity of love directed to our little community. But what struck me most was that the majority of notes came from children. They were simple, sweet, and heartbreakingly honest—like the crayon drawing by a first grader of a partially eaten pie surrounded by 26 burning birthday candles, with the message "Eat pie, it makes me feel better." Or the pink cardboard heart from schoolchildren in China that said, "Never give up! Keep a smile in your face, we love you forever!" And the poster from the African country of Liberia with paint handprints made by hundreds of children and the message "A Sympathy Card from the Children of Liberia to the Schoolchildren of Sandy Hook Elementary."

One letter was addressed to the North Pole and rerouted to Newtown by a thoughtful postal sorter—it was the Christmas list of a little girl named Skylar, and she'd written the only present she wanted from Santa was for him to visit the people in Sandy Hook and make them happy. Another girl from New Zealand wrote a poem and left her phone number at the bottom, just in case anyone in Sandy Hook "needed someone to talk to."

I was astounded by the compassion displayed by these children; and I shuddered when I read the notes from those who, like us, had also experienced violence in their lives. The students of Columbine High School sent a poster, reminding us that we were not alone and that their community was still healing 14 years after their own school massacre, which claimed the lives of

12 students and one teacher. In a letter pinned near that poster, a third grader from Illinois named Angela wrote, "I feel terrible about what happened. Who would do such a horrible thing? You should see how many shootings we have in Illinois! I am sending hope to you. I am sorry you had to face this."

And near that, a note from a small-town California girl named Jenna:

> To whoever is receiving this letter, I am terribly sorry about your loss. My thoughts are with you. My hometown, Seal Beach, went through a similar situation last year. We lost 12 lives that day. I will be sending you happy thoughts and prayers. I can't believe how hard this is for you. If this helps you, you can send me as many letters as you want, if you need someone to talk to, and comfort you through this horrible time. I am here for you. Sincerely yours, Jenna.

And our own mailbox at the farm was refilled each day with letters, notes, and poems offering us comfort, love, support, and encouragement. Just the thought that a person took the time to buy a card, write a few words, put a stamp on it, and mail it touches my heart. I now refer to all the sympathy cards we received as "love letters" because they are filled with such compassion. One day, a thick notebook arrived from a seventh-grade class in Alabama. The students in this class had read a newspaper story about how Jesse had helped his classmates, and in response they decided to perform random acts of kindness in his honor. I opened the notebook to find pages and pages describing simple deeds the students had done:

> "I visited my friend while he was sick."
> "I did the dishes for my mom."
> "I picked up a sheet of paper a student dropped."
> "I opened a girl's locker for her."

The children's heartfelt actions made me think of President Obama's speech in Sandy Hook two days after the tragedy. He had asked the country if we as a society were doing enough to protect our children. According to our President, the answer was no.

And he was right, we were not doing enough to protect our children and teach them how to care for and protect each other—not by a long shot. At that moment something clicked and my mission suddenly snapped into sharp focus. I needed to start a foundation to help kids realize the power they had to choose love over hate or anger.

Maybe, I thought, it is in our schools that Jesse's message would do the most good and have the greatest impact. Giving children the tools to cope with anger; helping them understand, control, and change their negative thoughts to positive ones; teaching them to treat others with kindness and respect—that was how I would shape my mission and bring Jesse's message to the world. And parents and teachers needed to hear this message, too. Now more than ever it was clear to me that we were all in this together.

. . .

Not long after that, as January drew to a close and the deepest days of winter set in, I paid a visit to Jesse's grave with a special gift for him. It was a box of "message stones" a friend of mine who'd passed away years earlier had left for me that I'd stowed in my closet, not sure of the right place to put them to use, until now. I picked out three stones from the bunch—"peace," "love," and "happiness" would be for Jesse. I kept "success," "health," and "luck" for myself and J.T., to help our healing and my newly focused mission.

I positioned the stones at the foot of Jesse's grave and told him all about my plans for the foundation that would carry his message. Afterward, I lay on the ground and made a snow angel next to Jesse's grave, hoping it would cheer up the next person who came by.

I think Jesse agreed with my plan, because when I got home J.T. and I sat down to rerecord some of his old phone messages for safekeeping, and the first one we heard was Jesse's exuberant voice saying, "Hey Mom, hey J.T. . . . let's *rock 'n' roll!*"

"You got it, Jesse. *You got it!*" I promised.

Right after that, two things happened that provided me with a name for the foundation I would organize and a forum to introduce that foundation to the world.

First, the village of Sandy Hook unofficially adopted a new motto that is the essence of nurturing, healing love and a validation of everything I had come to believe about my community and about the future: *We Are Sandy Hook, We Choose Love.*

The second was an invitation to speak in front of the Bipartisan Task Force on Gun Violence Prevention and Children's Safety, a group of state legislators assembled to examine if laws should be changed in the wake of the shooting. The focus of the meeting was school safety, mental health, and gun violence. It seemed an ideal place to publically announce what I planned to do.

A lot of parents of children who had been killed had signed up to speak at the meeting, as had other residents of Newtown touched by the shooting, so I knew there would likely be a debate over gun control. Many Sandy Hook parents had been actively lobbying for changes in state and federal gun laws, including Neil. As far as I saw it, all the parents were working toward the same goal—to create a safer world and to make sure something like this never happens again. But I wanted to focus my energies toward educating people about anger and violence, because to me the tragedy began as an angry thought in the shooter's mind.

My dad came to the meeting with me, and when we arrived I found out that I'd be the first family member to speak, following several officials. As I'd suspected, a passionate debate on restricting "assault-style" weapons began almost immediately and I became a bit uncomfortable. Could I talk about love when everyone else was arguing about guns?

I turned to my dad and said, "I'm not sure if this is the right forum to introduce Jesse's message. It's not the right place for me talk about nurturing, healing love." My dad put his hands on my shoulders and gave me a little shake. "Scarlett, this needs to be heard here tonight. This is the perfect place. It is important for everyone in this room to hear what you've come to say."

He was right. Before I spoke I put a few poster-sized photographs of Jesse up by the speaker's desk so everyone could see for themselves what kind of boy he was. Then I said a little prayer to set the tone and sat down in front of the microphone.

I told them about choosing love and about changing an angry thought to a loving one. And I told them what I had said at Jesse's funeral and the way it had changed the life of a 66-year-old doctor. And then I told them about the message Jesse had left me on the chalkboard—how it had changed me and why I believed it could help change the world and make it a better place for our children:

> I believe anger is a major issue in society. You do not use a gun against someone else unless you are angry, or a victim . . . Our children need to learn that they can choose love over anger, they can chose gratitude over entitlement, and in doing so can shape a happy and healthy future. If a child does not think he has control of his anger, over time he can become a victim. The majority of us can consciously choose between love and anger if we are aware we have the choice. You can choose between gratitude and entitlement.
>
> I am starting a foundation called the Jesse Lewis Choose Love Foundation. We will offer classes that teach children this awareness and that you do have a choice. This choice between anger and love is one that we all make when we wake up every morning. It is one we make at work, at home, with our children, on the road,

Spreading the word on Jesse's Choose Love Foundation

and in our schools. Most of us are probably not even aware we are making a choice.

Jesse wrote a message on our kitchen chalkboard sometime shortly before he died. The message was written in a six-year-old's handwriting and phonetically spelled, and said, "Nurturing Healing Love." This message of comfort and inspiration was for me, for my family, and for the world. The Jesse Lewis Choose Love Foundation is our way of turning anger in society into love. I hope you will support us in this effort as I truly believe we can, together, make the world a better place. Together we can turn this tragedy into the event that turned the tide, which empowered us as individuals, a society and world to choose love. Thank you.

When I finished I honestly didn't know what to expect. The room was so silent. I looked over to my father, and he was smiling at me with tears in his eyes. A second later, everyone in the room slowly rose from their chairs and began to clap, and clap—and clap. My eyes filled with tears, too.

I had just introduced Jesse's message to the world, and my little boy had gotten a standing ovation.

CHAPTER
NINE

Sharing
AND
Forgiving

No one gets a free pass when it comes to grief, and I sure wasn't an exception.

After such a positive response to my speech at the Bipartisan Task Force, I wanted to throw myself into building up the Foundation with all the energy I could muster, hoping I could shake off some of my sorrow and perhaps channel my grief toward my new mission. But it hadn't even been two months since Jesse's death, and some days it took all the energy I could muster just to get out of bed.

The grieving process, as I was learning, was not something that can be rushed or ignored. As Dr. Laura said to me during one of our sessions, "There is no other journey as unknown as grief. It is a way into the dark forest where nothing is familiar, and you have to manage your way through this landscape having lost your compass . . . yet, you must go through this darkness to reach the other side, to healing and even a spiritual rebirth. There is no other way out of the cocoon of grief but to break out."

One of my first difficult steps into that dark forest and of breaking out of my cocoon of grief was to meet with other parents who'd also lost children that day.

Within two weeks of the tragedy, some of the parents met for the first session of what would become a bimonthly (twice a month) support group. I missed the first meeting because I was in Orlando with J.T., but I made it to the second session—barely.

When I walked in, I was an hour late; and as soon as I caught sight of the gathering of grieving parents at the far end of the room, I burst into tears and ran into the bathroom. There I sat on the floor and cried for at least half an hour, until one of the grief counselors came to fetch me and bring me back. I wasn't sure I could handle being in that room. It was hard enough trying to handle my own grief; to be confronted with so many others as emotionally devastated as I was seemed utterly impossible. I was still sobbing when I entered the room for the second time. One of the fathers and several of the mothers—none of whom I knew beforehand—rushed over to hug me.

When I felt their arms around me I knew that coming to meet them had been the right decision. I had worried that being around so many parents with the same heartache as mine would magnify my pain, but that wasn't the case at all. By sharing our sorrow as a group, our own individual suffering lessened, if even just a little bit—and God knows, any relief was welcome. We bonded, and in that bond I found comfort. We soon called ourselves the Healing Hearts group, because that is what we became. Looking around the circle of parents I was sitting with, I knew there was no need to explain to them why I slept with Jesse's unwashed shirts on my pillow, why I needed to breathe in his scent, why I hated to walk into a supermarket where I felt the eyes of strangers watching my every move and expression, or why I looked for signs from Jesse wherever I was or whatever I was doing—these people, my new friends and co-grievers, already understood . . . they got it.

The cost of membership in our group was so painfully high that I wish I could say we were the only ones—but we weren't. And thankfully, those who had lived through similar nightmares and survived the same kind of senseless, violent tragedies reached out to offer us their comfort, encouragement, and advice.

In fact, one of the first things we did as a group was to have a conference call with parents who'd lost children in the Columbine High School massacre of 1999, the Virginia Tech shooting in 2007, and the movie-theater shooting in Aurora, Colorado, which happened just five months before Sandy Hook.

"Look around you," one of the Columbine parents said to us over the phone. "These people are going to be your main support system for the rest of your life, so get to know them. Use every opportunity you can to get together with them, because this is it."

For many of us, it was a challenge just to stay alive those first few weeks. To be totally honest, the thought of suicide fleetingly crossed my mind during that first month, and I understood now why some people do it. The pain was so great, and the situation so irreversible, at times it was difficult to imagine going on. On one of those early days, I sat at my computer and composed a letter to J.T. telling him that if I died, I wanted him to know how much I loved him and how he'd be okay and that I'd always be with him. I had gotten only halfway through the letter when it spontaneously erased, right in front of my eyes. I think Jesse didn't like the idea of me writing a letter like that. He wanted to protect his brother and erased it so that J.T. would never, ever see it. And he was also telling me, "No way, Mom!"

As painful as grief gets, how would I ever explain to Jesse or J.T. that I just gave up? We'd seen so many examples of strength in hard times that I couldn't possibly make that choice. When Jesse was alive, we often went to visit a friend named Bobby, who is in a wheelchair with ALS. No matter what he was going through, he never gave up, and Jesse loved him for this optimism. After Jesse passed, J.T. and I went to visit Bobby. His condition had progressed to the point where he was having trouble talking and swallowing. And even then, before we left the hospital, he looked me in the eye and whispered, "Never stop living. Don't ever give up—*never* give up!" I looked right back at Bobby and promised him I wouldn't.

At Healing Hearts, not only do we cry together but we also, thank God, laugh together—often at the insanity of our situation and at details no one outside our group would find funny at all.

"The other day a very sweet old lady said to me that she knew how I felt losing my son because she had lost her dog a few years earlier," I shared with the group one night. "I smiled and nodded understandingly to her . . . but I just wanted to punch her in the face!"

We all laughed until we cried at the absurdity of that one.

I feel blessed that I have had the opportunity to get to know these other parents, and that I've been able to open up so they could get to know me. It has been comforting to compare notes on our grief over the months and be able to help each other deal with situations that, even in the furthest reaches of our imaginations, we'd never thought we'd confront. Like what to do with our children's toys and clothes (some parents were making quilts using their child's shirts and pants and coats), or how to react when the school bus slows down in front of your house to pick up your child, and then suddenly speeds away once the bus driver remembers the child they used to pick up is no longer there.

It didn't take long to realize that anger, like my wanting to punch out someone, was part of our pain, and part of the anger was not being able to forgive. Forgive whom? Well, first we had to forgive ourselves. I've learned that whenever a parent loses a child so suddenly, they can become wracked with guilt—which, at least for me, is anger at myself—for things I did or didn't do. It's natural to feel guilt for every ice-cream cone denied or every scolding given, feeling as if I'd not been a good enough mother and knowing that it's too late to make up for those shortcomings. Thank God I had made that decision early on to appreciate every moment of time with my boys, to kiss that cheek every chance I got, so I know I gave Jesse as much love and attention as I possibly could. And yet, for the first two months after Jesse's death, I was haunted by one memory in particular—I had given him a rare time-out that lasted longer than it probably should have. It was so minor, but it haunted me.

It took me time and some therapy to realize that the reason I kept replaying it over and over in my mind was that I hadn't forgiven myself for it. I also knew that in order to move forward and heal I would have to let go of my guilt—I would have to forgive myself and accept that I'd been the best mother I had been able to be at that time.

"These thoughts will show up and they will torture us," I said to the group, "and we can choose to indulge them or we can choose to let them go and try to replace them with a happier memory. That's what I've been trying to do, and it helps. It's not always easy. There's no magical fix. And it's something you have to do every day, choosing more positive and loving thoughts. Especially for us, it might be a lifelong struggle. But it will help us heal, help us find some peace and find the spark of joy remaining inside of us."

Forgiving yourself is one thing—forgiving the person who killed your child is something else entirely. To many, that would seem like an impossible, impossible task. For me, I believe I had been preparing for it since Jesse was born.

At one point during my spiritual journey, I'd read Immaculée Ilibagiza's book *Left to Tell*. This was not long after I gave birth to Jesse. It's the story of how the author's family was slaughtered along with a million others during the 1994 Rwandan genocide, and about how she herself survived, healed from the trauma, and then forgave the killers who murdered her family. Near the end of the book, she visits her mother's killer in prison and the warden gives her permission to take whatever revenge she wants on the murderer, who lay chained and helpless at her feet.

With Immaculée, whose book inspired me
to forgive.

She could have spit on him, kicked him, even *killed*
him if she wanted to, but instead she looked into his
eyes, touched his hands, and said, "I forgive you."
Later, she explains that she could not live with hatred
in her heart and that if she wanted to be happy, her
only choice was to choose love by forgiving the man.
She added that forgiveness was the only way to end
the cycle of anger and hatred that had led to the genocide in the first place.

When I read the scene where she forgives her
mother's murderer, I remember admiring her compassion, but also thinking I could *never* forgive someone
who killed my family, especially if it was one of my
children. Now, six years later, I was facing a similar situation and, along with so many other parents, I was
confronted with a similar choice.

Some people in Sandy Hook had such anger toward the young man in question that they wouldn't even utter his name, Adam Lanza. Not only do they remain unspeakably angry at him, but also at his mother, Nancy, whom he also killed that day.

People automatically assume I'm angry at Adam as well. And I admit, I've had a few moments when I am enraged, moments when I wish he could feel the same pain and hurt he inflicted on our children and on us. But the truth is I have not felt a lot of anger toward him—and I know that shocks a lot of people. But as soon as I'd learned what Adam had done, I immediately thought that there had to be something very, very wrong with him—no person in his right mind could have committed such a heinous act. And if he was severely disturbed, I could not hold on to anger toward him—I would have to forgive him, which I did. Since then I have been told that perhaps Adam had been struggling with emotional or mental problems since childhood and was also horribly bullied as a child, although I still avoid reading news reports about the shooting and am unsure of the details or extent of Adam's problems.

I am not looking for excuses, but I am looking for reasons—and I can see how his own emotional turmoil and anger at being a victim would have played a role in his victimizing our children so viciously. By understanding what went wrong for Adam, I hope we can prevent the same kind of horrendous violence from occurring in the future—that is my goal.

I used to talk to J.T. and Jesse about finding compassion, practicing forgiveness, and trying to understand the pain others might be experiencing that made them lash out in anger. Even in *Rose's Foal*, the mama horse tells the colt that we must put ourselves "in someone else's horseshoes to understand how they feel."

So when people ask me how I can forgive the man who killed my child, I say, "Hating Adam will not bring Jesse back. It will only hurt me and generate more anger and hatred."

When we forgive someone, we do it for everyone.

We do it for the whole world, and for our future. We do it for our children. But mostly, we do it for ourselves.

CHAPTER TEN | Trauma AND Looking Within

Prayer has always comforted me. After the tragedy, when I needed comforting more than ever before, I prayed more than ever before. But it wasn't something new to me. Praying has always been a way for me and my boys to look beyond ourselves to express gratitude for our many gifts and to seek guidance and help, but it was also a way of looking within to create a stillness in our hearts and bring peace and calmness to our hectic lives.

Prayer to me is a way to acknowledge that there is a higher being and a master plan, and that I am loved unconditionally.

My prayers used to be directed mostly to God and his heavenly son, Jesus. But ever since my mystical foot-washing ceremony with Dr. Laura, I have added Mother Mary to my prayers. Mary was a mother with a mother's heart that had been shattered like mine. Once I began praying to Mary for solace, I felt her near to me at all times, like a gentle hand on my shoulder helping me through my sorrow.

I also began reading another of Immaculée's books, *Our Lady of Kibeho*, and started praying the Rosary of the Seven Sorrows, one of the prayers Immaculée says helped her through her own grief. The Seven Sorrows represent the major sorrows Mary suffered after the birth of Jesus—like his torture and execution. When I prayed this rosary, I both identified with Mary's anguish and was comforted that she, too, knew mine. For me, Mary symbolizes the suffering of all mothers who have lost a child. My growing connection with her, and my new understanding of the grace and quietness in which she mourned, helped (and continues to help) me in my grief.

I also wanted the comfort that a prayerful community could provide—but it was so very hard for me to walk into a church service. The fear of collapsing into a sobbing mess when confronted by all the concerned faces and encouraging words of well-meaning parishioners had kept me from the Sunday sermons that I hoped would inspire me and lift my spirits.

Then one Sunday morning I was feeling especially in need of a spiritual boost, and I mustered up the courage to try to attend a service. I got as far as the church parking lot. My neighbor Roberta was inside, hoping I'd join her in her family pew, but instead I sat in my car and cried. Finally I texted her: I CAN'T DO IT, ROBERTA. CAN YOU COME BY MY PLACE LATER AND WE CAN DO SOME BIBLE READING TOGETHER?

I put the keys back into the ignition and said a prayer to Mary for help and guidance, and a thought popped into my head: *I am exactly the kind of person who Jesus welcomes into the church—the broken of spirit.* I also figured that the sermon had already started by now and I could slip in unnoticed and sit in the back by the sanctuary, where I would be by myself. So I went in and sat alone and listened to the pastor, but I wasn't relating to the sermon at all. I picked up the Sunday bulletin—bad move—and saw a notice to parents about Sunday school for the kids, the same class Jesse loved attending. I burst into tears.

Right on cue, Roberta appeared and sat down beside me with a box of tissues. She handed me one and started flipping through the pages of her Bible.

"I know you came today hoping to hear something that would help you, and you think you haven't," she said, "so look at this."

She passed the opened Bible to me and pointed to Romans 12:2, which is a passage about changing your thoughts. It was exactly what I needed to read: "Do not conform to the pattern of this world, but be transformed by the renewing of your mind. Then you will be able to test and approve what God's will is—his good, pleasing, and perfect will."

I had been slowly working my way through grief with my Healing Hearts parent group, as well as seeing Dr. Laura and going to more conventional therapy sessions—but I knew I had to go deeper. After the tragedy, violent images had begun flashing through my mind at all times of the day and night . . . and they were getting progressively worse.

So in February, I began a strange and wonderful journey into the world of "alternative" therapies that led me onto brand new roads.

First I tried Reiki, which Ashly had suggested to me. It was a kind of "laying on of the hands" developed by a Japanese monk, she explained, that unblocked the "life force energy" in a person and got it flowing again. I got on the table and closed my eyes and the Reiki master started moving her hands above me but didn't touch me. I felt chills run down my spine, and then a warm, flowing energy that travelled all around my body.

At one point I felt as if my mind and spirit were rocketing into outer space. I passed "beings" made entirely of light and realized that they were the souls of the children from the school. Then I passed beyond them, feeling like my physical body was levitating from the table as I continued moving deeper into space. I saw a ring of blurred stars surrounding a great black circle, which I thought might be the entrance to heaven, and I wondered if that was where I was headed. I wouldn't have minded at all, because it was so very peaceful. When I opened my eyes I still felt at peace, and that sense of well-being stayed with me for days.

That same week I tried hypnosis for the first time.

I had made an appointment with Judith, an empowerment coach I'd seen six years earlier when I was making big changes in my life after Jesse was born. One of the things I loved about her was that she was very spiritual, but she was also very assertive about a person's healing. At the end of my past sessions, she always gave me "homework." I felt like I wanted and needed Judith's strong approach now in order to heal. Judith came over to my house, and we wasted no time in getting down to business.

"Tell me what to do," I said to her, "so that I can move forward. Just tell me what to do and I'll do it."

She told me my hypnosis could take me in several different directions, and she presented me with a few options, including one in which I might be able to see and communicate with Jesse.

"I choose that one," I said without hesitation.

I lay on the couch and closed my eyes, and Judith immediately brought me into a relaxed hypnotic state. Within a few minutes, I could see Jesse's face in such incredibly sharp detail that it was as if he was standing in front of me. I was so excited! It was the first time since he'd died that I'd experienced anything so detailed about him. Suddenly I felt myself moving through a dark tunnel that ended in a circle of kaleidoscopic color where I saw Jesse's face again, as well as the faces of many other children who were surrounding him. Jesse looked like he always did in life—happy, smiling, and laughing. The other children were laughing as well, and I was very happy that Jesse had so many playmates and that he was having "a lot of fun." I woke up from the session with an incredible sense of relief! I felt wonderful, as if I actually saw him and that he was as happy as could be. *Jesse!*

This was a happy image, Judith reminded me, that I could flood my mind with the next time one of those other upsetting ones flashed in front of my eyes.

But even that relief didn't end or soften the jagged and painfully graphic images of the shooting that kept appearing in my mind, haunting both my waking hours and my sleep. A family friend and veteran who had recently returned from war and was plagued by the same type of horrid mental pictures recommended that I seek the help of a post-traumatic stress disorder (PTSD) specialist. He had done this and been treated with a technique known as eye movement desensitization and reprocessing (EMDR), which is a form of psychotherapy often used to treat soldiers or anyone who is suffering from post-traumatic stress.

I had no idea what to expect as I drove to my first appointment with the therapist, whose name was Sherri Rainingbird. When I got to her office, I described in detail the sudden, terrifying flashes of extreme violence that were bombarding me. I also told her about the emotional anguish and stabbing physical pain I woke up with every morning, and that I needed sleeping pills to knock me out and keep me out at night.

"You have classic symptoms of post-traumatic stress disorder," she said. "It's the same trauma soldiers often experience after combat."

She explained that my mind and body were stuck in a state of panicked expectation, that's why I woke up feeling like I was strapped into a speeding car seconds away from slamming into a brick wall. And, with the amount of adrenaline being continually pumped into my body, she said, it was little wonder I had trouble sleeping.

"We're going to reprogram your brain," Sherri said.

She instructed to me to relax, breathe deeply, and think about the upsetting images that plagued me while following the finger she waved from side to side in front of me with my eyes.

I imagined the school hallway on the day of the shooting . . . and then shooter with the gun . . . and then red, blood everywhere, all I could see was red . . .

"What do you see?" she asked.

I told her—all the while following her constantly moving finger—left, right, left, right, until everything began to blur and I had to shut my eyes. When I opened them, we started again, but this time the red that had blotted out everything the first time occupied only the bottom half of the image in my mind. We repeated the exercise several times—deep, regular breathing; visualizing; following her finger; closing and reopening eyes. Then at one point something remarkable happened: the image that had upset me so badly had vanished and been replaced by something completely different.

"I see a bright light coming from above," I told Sherri. "And I see all the children, like little spirits, flying up through this beautiful tunnel of light."

Sherri kept waving her finger from side to side and told me to shut my eyes and describe what I saw again.

What I saw startled me—it looked like the dark figure in the school drawing Jesse had made just before he was killed, the drawing in which Jesse had given himself angel wings and had scribbled over the face of the menacing figure he was confronting.

"There is a dark figure," I said.

"Who is it?"

"It's Adam. I still see the bright light; it's above him."

"What do you want to happen with the dark figure?" Sherri asked.

"I'd like for him to go to the light, to go through the tunnel, where the children went."

"Then have him do that," she said.

And I did. I imagined the dark figure ascending toward the tunnel until the light enveloped him. My mind flooded with an intense, brilliant white light, and when I opened my eyes I knew that something had changed inside of me. When I closed my eyes again, I saw an image of a white, luminescent cross suspended in space. I looked at Sherri; I was practically speechless—it was a profound healing experience. I had just exchanged the worst thought I had ever imagined into something light and beautiful. After that session, the images that had tortured me for weeks dwindled to just a few minor, fleeting thoughts.

When I left Sherri's, I was buzzing with a new lightness of being. I drove to the cemetery to meet up with J.T., Dad, Mom, and Bob so we could watch Ned the Tombstone Guy lower the site marker onto Jesse's grave. The marker had a little duck and an angel carved into the corners, and little soldiers engraved along the bottom. It read:

> *We are so proud of*
>
> *Jesse McCord Lewis*
>
> *"Have a lot of Fun"*

Amazingly, I smiled when I saw the marker and how sweet it was. I also smiled when I saw my parents standing side by side, which was a minor miracle. They hadn't crossed paths or spoken to each other since their divorce more than 25 years earlier. For a quarter of a century, they carefully coordinated any comings and goings at college graduations, weddings, holidays, birthdays, and the births of their grandchildren so they would never have to see each other. But here they were today, coming together to support J.T. and me—and Jesse.

Soldiers, a duck, and an angel engraved on Jesse's grave marker

And that was progress; that was healing. Thank you, Jesse!

I could feel myself beginning to heal, too. I had lifted my head up a few inches above the darkness of despair, and I could see a little bit of light in the distance.

I put my arm around J.T.'s shoulder as Ned caringly made a few final adjustments to Jesse's marker. I had found my own healing path and was on my way, but after several failed attempts at therapy that only left him frustrated, J.T. hadn't found his yet. He was suffering, I could see that, but I didn't know how to help him.

Thank God help was on its way and would soon arrive with a knock on our farmhouse door.

PART IV | MOVING
FORWARD

CHAPTER
ELEVEN

HeLPing HAnDS

As I felt my trauma ease little by little, I was able to move forward little by little.

Soon the day came when I was able to give away Jesse's bunk beds—it was a huge step for me. He had inherited them practically new from J.T. and had barely used them, so I gave them to a dear friend who had two sons whom Jesse really liked—he would have approved. Before the beds went to their new home, I found some of Jesse's little toys and a pair of pajamas stuck in the sides of the mattress. It was like finding a little gift.

That day, my friend Jen had come to help me sort through some of Jesse's things and all the boxes of letters and cards that were stacked up all over the house. We were chatting about the alternative therapies I was looking into, when she asked me if I'd ever heard about "tapping."

I had. Tapping, also known as Emotional Freedom Technique (EFT), is a combination of acupressure and psychology in which you tap on main energy points of your body with your finger while saying positive affirmations out loud. The goal is to overcome negative thought patterns or feelings and replace them with positive ones. I'd tried it a few years earlier to see if it would help me make some extra money and lose some extra weight, but I didn't see any immediate results at the time so I had lost interest.

"Well if you want to try it again," Jen told me, "I can arrange to have Nick Ortner at your house *tonight.*"

Nick was a well-known expert on tapping, and as it turns out he lived in Newtown and had been doing tapping sessions in Sandy Hook since that terrible December day. Jen knew a friend of Nick's, and so a few hours later, Nick and his colleague Dr. Lori Leyden, a psychotherapist and tapping practitioner, were on my doorstep.

Within a couple of minutes we were chatting like old friends. Nick joked that he felt right at home, noting all the motivational books scattered around the living room, many of which were from the same publisher that was about to release Nick's book. Our connection was immediate.

As I often say, I don't believe in coincidences, so I know that meeting Nick and Lori that night was no coincidence—they both had been brought into my life for a reason, and not only to help me heal. I had a feeling Jesse had brought them into our living room for another reason as well, and I smiled . . . waiting for it all to unfold.

That's when Lori noticed I was reading Immaculée's books. She told me she'd spent much of the past five years in Rwanda helping genocide survivors who were children at the time of the massacre and were now young adults and still struggling with the trauma. Many had witnessed their parents being slaughtered and had been left to fend for themselves; most never continued with school and had to raise their even younger siblings all by themselves.

Talk about trauma. J.T. and I had the help of family and friends—loved ones who brought food to our door, prepared our meals, managed the farm, and took J.T. to movies and the arcade and out riding dirt bikes. These Rwandan kids were trying to put their lives back together with *nothing*—well, almost nothing.

"You would be amazed at how a little love and compassion and the right resources can totally transform the lives of even those who were that severely traumatized," Lori said. I could see that J.T. was very shaken up by her descriptions of what she had witnessed or heard about in Rwanda. But it was soon time to do our first tapping session, so we changed the course of the discussion.

Before we began, Nick explained how it worked. When our thoughts focus on a traumatic event, he said, it triggers the amygdala, the part of our brain that releases stress hormones for our fight-or-flight response. So if we get stuck focusing on traumas from the past or present, we live in a perpetual state of stress and fear. Tapping sends a calming signal to the brain, telling us that we are no longer in danger, that we're safe. And because we talk aloud about the trauma we suffered while we are tapping on our body's energy points, we are able to retrain our brain and change the way a traumatic event affects us. In other words, we begin to heal.

Nick and I sat next to each other on the couch, and he asked me to relax, shut my eyes, and verbalize the event or feeling causing me the most stress. My dad and J.T. were in the room with us, and we all expected that I would start talking about the trauma at the firehouse or my sadness at losing Jesse. But as soon as my eyes closed, neither of those feelings came to me. My fingers curled up and clenched into the palms of my hands.

"How do you feel?" Nick asked, noticing my fists.

"I'm *angry!*"

"Okay . . ." Nick said. "Who are you angry at?"

I surprised myself by telling Nick about a small transgression someone had committed that had upset me. I imagine everyone in the room was glancing at each other in surprise, but my eyes were closed, so I couldn't say for sure. I had the country's leading tapping expert in my living room and the trauma I chose to explore was some small offense and not the loss of my precious son from one of the worst mass shootings in the history of America? What the heck was that all about?

Nick is a genius when it comes to emotions, and he saw right through my anger. Perhaps, he suggested, I was focusing on this anger right now to prevent me from fully facing the reality of Jesse's death? Perhaps, he suggested, I could also forgive this person and move on?

I opened my eyes and looked up at him as I kept tapping on the energy point on the top of my head. Then I smiled.

He was absolutely correct. I had managed to forgive the man who'd killed my son—but I was walking around with a grudge over a much lesser grievance like it was a knife stuck in my chest.

Nick had just reminded me of one of the most

Tapping expert Nick Ortner helped me heal from trauma.

important truths about forgiveness: it is an act we do for ourselves. So we tapped through my anger at this person, and when we were done . . . it was gone and I was over it! Now, Nick said, I was free to deal with the bigger issues. Or as Dr. Laura might say, it was time to get down to the sacred act of grieving—and healing.

Lori came to my house on her own for my next tapping session. She explained to me that my trauma and grief had to be treated separately, in the same way we'd dealt with my anger in the session before. To get to the grief we first had to peel away at the trauma one layer at a time. I was still in physical shock at losing Jesse, she said, which produced chemicals that were coating my grief and making it even more difficult to process. Her wisdom resonated with me, and I was very impressed because she was the only therapist who had explored that issue with me.

It took a few sessions of peeling away at the layers before Nick and I finally arrived at the day of the shooting, the day at the firehouse. I tapped through the trauma of that day and then . . . another surprise. As Nick gently nudged me further and further into the emotions I had experienced that day, we reached a place in my mind and in my heart that was still *hopeful* that none of what I'd experienced was true. Even though I had been told Jesse was gone and had seen him in his casket and held his cold hand in mine, I was still clinging to the hope that it was all some big mistake.

Hope in itself is a good thing, maybe the best of all things. But not when it blocks us from the reality we must face. In order to heal I had to come to a place of *acceptance*.

So Nick and I tapped together and acknowledged that Jesse was not coming back, that his body was dead, and that I fully accepted this fact.

"I feel a pain in my chest," I told Nick, "like I swallowed a stone and it's lodged in my heart."

"Let's tap the stone out of your heart," Nick said, "and replace it with a feather."

We tapped that, yes, Jess might be physically dead, but his soul was in heaven and his spirit was also all around me. And we tapped that I knew I would see him again one day. We tapped that I did not *believe* this to be true—I *knew* it to be true. I knew it as solidly and surely as I knew I loved Jesse and J.T. When we had finished and I opened my eyes, I felt an incredible lightness of spirit.

Nick and Lori would tap with me regularly over the coming months to help me continue to heal. J.T. sat in on a few of our sessions, watching with a mixture of curiosity, dubiousness, and amusement. After much coaxing, he gave tapping a try, but it wasn't for him just yet. He wasn't ready to talk about his most troubling memories and thoughts with others, and that's why traditional therapy wasn't working for him, either. He'd tried a few different therapists; but I soon saw how uncomfortable it was for him to open up, and I understood that it wasn't the right healing method for him.

But what was? It had been months since Jesse's death and J.T. still wasn't going to school regularly and had become increasingly withdrawn and angry; one time he even punched a hole in the wall of his bedroom.

I thought about how confusing J.T.'s emotions must be surrounding his brother's death, and remembered the words he'd written as a eulogy for Jesse, which Trent read out loud at the funeral:

> Brothers fight, brothers hate, but most important—brothers love. I loved my brother and he loved me. We could only express that in short video game playing or maybe a small game of soccer. I would

get him off the bus and fix him food. He would say I have homework, and I would say I have video games. For years I thought I hated my brother, but I didn't. My brother died helping little kids like him try and escape the school. I believe he left this world to see them through. He was very brave, too. Our house has two floors, like all young kids he had a fear of the dark lifeless upstairs. But he would go up anyway. I love my brother.

The boys had a normal big-brother-little-brother relationship that included the usual little-brother-annoying-big-brother moments and the usual big-brother-yelling-at-little-brother moments. But now that Jesse was gone, I knew that J.T. felt some guilt, in the same way that many parents might, thinking that sometimes he'd been too hard on Jesse.

Lori had picked up on J.T.'s distress early on, and one night told me she had an idea how to help him. When she had first begun talking about the work she did in Rwanda helping with genocide survivors, J.T. had been fascinated. So she grabbed onto this light she had seen in him and started talking more about her story and about how she ended up founding Project LIGHT: Rwanda. Lori told us that several years ago she'd been hospitalized for three weeks with an illness so severe that she had a profound near-death experience that led to a new "soul" purpose.

"When I woke up, I made a decision to follow my heart, wherever that led," Lori said.

Lori had reached J.T. He wanted to know everything

about the kids Lori was working with in Rwanda. And before we knew it, Lori had set up a live Skype session for J.T. to talk to two of her Project LIGHT ambassadors in Rwanda.

A few of us, including Lori, Jen, Dad, and me, watched over J.T.'s shoulder as he introduced himself to Chantal and Mathieu who, with the help of an interpreter, began the conversation by offering condolences to J.T.

"We heard about Newtown here in Rwanda, and we are so sorry. We know that you lost your little brother, and our hearts break for you," Chantal said to him.

"We want you to know that we love you and that we are praying for you," Mathieu added.

Chantal shared her story first. She was now 26, but had been just 7 years old when the genocide swept across Rwanda. "They came with machetes and they killed my entire family and all my neighbors right in front of me. Then they grabbed me by the hair and slit my throat; they cut me all over my body. They buried me in a shallow grave with my family, but I dug myself out. I hid by the dead bodies. My family was dead, and I was taken to an orphanage. I had no friends and very little food."

Chantal showed us the scars on her neck, back, arms, and legs and said it took years for her physical wounds to heal, and that her emotional and psychological wounds really only began to heal after meeting Lori and learning the tools to overcome her trauma. Looking at this sweet, articulate young woman who had sparkling eyes and radiated a peaceful, contented aura, it was difficult to connect her with the nightmare story she was telling us.

"And now I am here to tell you that through faith and forgiveness and tapping, I've been able to heal," she said with a smile. "I know you must be angry, J.T. I was angry, too. But healing is possible. You are going to be okay, J.T."

Mathieu was as openhearted as Chantal, and his story just as difficult (and just as inspiring) to hear. Now 23, he was 4 years old when the genocide began. For the 100 days that the genocide raged around him, Mathieu eluded the killers who were hunting him by hiding with a few others in the tall grass near his village. That grass was all he had to eat for three months as he watched from a distance as his friends and relatives were brutally murdered. Mathieu's mother died, and his father went mad from grief and the overwhelming trauma of the genocide. Mathieu was left to care for his father and three siblings.

Yet despite everything he went through, he still dreamed of getting an education because it was the only way to lift his family out of poverty. He dreamed of going to college one day even though it seemed impossible, and now he was a student at the Kigali Institute of Education.

"My urge to go to school was so great that I walked two hours in the morning down a mountain to get to the school, and then two hours back up the mountain to get home. I had no money and could not afford to eat breakfast or lunch . . . but that was my dream and now I am doing it! We helped each other get better and found out how to get through it all together. And you will get through this, too, J.T."

We were awestruck at the bravery and resilience of these two precious people and couldn't quite believe that anyone could overcome such horror, hardship, and pain—even worse than our own—to be so happy. J.T. and I had help and comforts during our grief—friends and family who brought us food and solace and a warm bed and home to sleep in. Chantal and Mathieu had nothing.

They were truly inspirational.

And no one was more inspired than J.T. Later that night I found him in his room scribbling furiously in a notebook, and I asked him what he was writing about so passionately.

"I'm putting together a fund-raising project for the kids from the genocide; I want to help send them to college. I'm going to school tomorrow to get started."

School?! I couldn't have been prouder—or more relieved. J.T. had found a mission that would become his "soul purpose." And being of service and helping others would be his way to help himself and start to heal.

J.T. returned to school the next day and spent the coming weeks working with his pals Alex and Jordan researching the genocide, making presentations to his classmates and teachers, and organizing fund-raising drives. He even went around town handing out colorful rubber wristbands stamped with the phrase "Newtown Helps Rwanda."

J.T. threw himself into his project with the same dedication and passion I was devoting to Jesse's Choose Love Foundation, and the positive change in his attitude was incredible to see.

Soon, he and his friends had raised the $1,600 needed to pay the first-year tuition for a 26-year-old Rwandan woman named Betty, who was a 7-year-old during the genocide and had been left on her own

J.T. (with Dr. Lori Leyden) Skyping with his new Rwandan friends

to take care of her eight siblings. He also raised an additional $500 so Betty could support her family and cover her living expenses while she'd be away studying.

After J.T. announced that he'd reached his first fund-raising goal, Lori came over to the house and set up another Skype session so J.T. and Alex could tell Betty the good news face-to-face.

"Betty!" J.T. told her. "I'm sending you to university!"

When the interpreter in Rwanda translated J.T.'s words, Betty's beautiful face lit up, her hands flew to her cheeks, and she doubled over in shock. When she was able to look up at J.T.'s face on her screen, she was crying. "Thank you," she whispered. "Thank you, thank you, thank you . . ."

A smile spread across J.T.'s entire face. He was happy—happier than he'd been in months, and so was I.

After the Skype session, J.T. and Alex ran outside—Alex jumped onto his dirt bike, and J.T. hopped onto an ATV. I watched through the kitchen window as they tore around the farm, stirring up a dust storm and terrorizing the chickens—the boys out conquering the world, having a lot of fun. It was so, so great.

CHAPTER TWELVE | FinDing a Voice for Change

A few weeks after J.T. met the two Rwandan genocide survivors who inspired him with their faith, courage, and resilience, I met two people whose strength and wisdom have been inspiring me for years—Louise Hay and Wayne Dyer.

The invitation came from Nick, who was speaking about tapping at a conference in New York City that was being put on by Hay House, his publisher. Both Louise and Wayne would be there, and I was thrilled when Nick took me along with him and Lori to meet Louise on the eve of the conference. My impression of her was just as I expected: She was a beautiful, graceful presence—a very special lady. She listened and smiled knowingly when I told her that her book *You Can Heal Your Life* had helped me do just that.

That night Lori and I checked into the Leo House, a Christian guesthouse in Manhattan where travelling nuns and priests often stay when passing through New York. As we walked into the hotel, I was reminded both of my mission and of the importance of being of service to others by the House's motto, prominently displayed on a gold plaque in the main lobby: *What we do for ourselves dies with us. What we do for others and the world remains and is immortal.*

The next morning, we took our seats in the auditorium of the conference center along with three thousand other people who were awaiting Wayne Dyer's arrival onstage. Wayne was the keynote speaker, and he was scheduled to talk for three hours, which didn't seem like much time considering the depth and breadth of the knowledge he'd amassed through years studying the world's most learned philosophers and spiritual leaders. I admired Wayne's passion for life, his love of humanity, and his insights into how we can all live happier and more soulful lives. Just before the seminar was to start I heard Wayne's familiar voice over the PA system doing a testing-one-two-three sound check. I was so excited, I reached into my pocket and squeezed one of Jesse's army men that I'd brought with me—I never leave home without a little something of Jesse's to help keep me focused on my mission. Suddenly Nick appeared beside me in the aisle. He'd just been up front telling Wayne all about Jesse.

"Wayne wants to meet you."

Nick took my hand and escorted me to a flight of stairs that led up to the stage. When I reached the top step I found Wayne standing there waiting for me, his arms stretched out wide in welcome and one of the kindest smiles I'd ever seen spread across his beaming face. I walked right into his bear hug as he asked me, "Do you feel him?"

Those were Wayne's first words to me, and it was

typical of him, I'd soon learn—skip the formalities and cut right to the heart of the matter.

"Absolutely!" I replied. "He is with me everywhere."

"I could feel him coming up the steps with you. I feel him all around us."

"Yes, I know." I smiled.

They were already adjusting the lights in the auditorium, a signal for Wayne to get onstage and begin his seminar.

"Would you like to say a few words to the audience?"

"Sure!" I answered, without thinking twice. I naturally assumed that Jesse had arranged this opportunity to share his message, and who was I to pass it up?

Obviously I hadn't prepared anything to say; the last thing I expected when I woke up that morning—or even five minutes beforehand—was that I would speak in front of 3,000 people in a packed Manhattan convention center.

"Are you nervous?" Nick asked, looking nervous himself.

"Actually, not really . . ."

"Well, do you want to tap about being nervous, just in case?"

"Maybe that would be a good idea," I said.

So we began tapping right there; he started and I followed his lead. Then Nick said the first phrase I was to repeat: "I feel good about this, even though I'm nervous and about to throw up on stage in front of thousands of people . . ."

We both cracked up. Nick had just taught me another lesson—it's impossible to belly laugh *and* be nervous at the same time. Like I said, Nick is a genius when it comes to working through emotions. And as it turns out, he's also a bit of a techno-wizard. Just before I walked onstage he asked if I had any pictures of Jesse with me.

"Yeah . . . they're all on this," I said, holding up my phone.

Nick grabbed my phone and hurried off. A couple of minutes later I was standing center stage as Wayne introduced me to his audience and then stepped aside to let me speak. I looked out into the giant auditorium; and with nothing prepared, I spoke from a mother's heart.

I started out by telling them that my Sweet Boy of Joy was born brave and sweet and loving, and with cheeks so irresistible they had to be kissed, and often. I told them about his strength and compassion. And about his incredible courage that never once deserted him, not even when he was facing death—and that he chose to save his friends instead of running for his life. I told them everything I've told you about Jesse throughout these pages, about how he came into the world big and that even now, after his death, his spirit is such a force that he's able to write us messages in the sky. I told them about his tender "I Love You" good-bye message to me on my car window, and that his soul knew he was going to leave.

It was at that point that I noticed people glancing up at something above my head. When I took a quick peek over my shoulder, I saw Jesse's little face bathed in light and his silly, toothy grin smiling back at me from a giant screen. Nick had hooked up my phone to a projector and was displaying images of Jesse synced up perfectly with the stories I was telling—the picture of the "I Love You" etched in frost, Jesse's drawing from

Center stage in New York with Wayne Dyer

school of him as a little angel confronting a bad man, and a picture of his chalkboard message: Norurting helin love.

I don't know how long I spoke, but I do know that I ended by talking about choices: How happy I was that I'd chosen to show my boys that I love them with every opportunity I had, and with every word and action. And also about the vitally important choice we all could make every day—to choose love in all we do, for our own sake, for the sake of our children, and for the sake of the world. A choice so important, in fact, that I had vowed to dedicate the rest of my life to helping people make it, and I invited them all to band together to help make this world one filled with compassion.

It was the second time I'd spoken publically about Jesse's message, and it was the second time my boy received a standing ovation.

Twenty-four hours later, I was walking barefoot along the ocean's edge in the Virgin Islands, still floating on that wave of love back in Manhattan.

I'd come with J.T. to St. Thomas for a few days during his February school break, and we met Trent and his family there. They'd rented a beautiful house with a deck and a private beach. J.T. loved hanging out with my brothers; they gave him a good dose of male uncle energy and attention. And I loved getting away someplace sunny and distant to catch my breath and reflect on everything from a different perspective. As I walked along the beach, I thought about how far J.T. and I had come in the past couple of months, and how far yet we had to go.

We were still grieving and our healing process was really just beginning—but the important thing was that it had begun. We had reached out to others and others had reached back to us. I was making every effort to heal my mind and body to be present for J.T., and both of us were doing service for others—J.T. with his fund-raising for the young Rwandans, and me with the Choose Love Foundation. The response to my impromptu speech confirmed to me my commitment to spread the foundation's message and move forward with my mission.

.   .   .

As always, I felt Jesse's presence all around me—but it seemed especially strong strolling down that beautiful beach where I could so easily picture him running barefoot in the sand next to me and fearlessly plunging into the cold surf. Jesse and I used to walk along the beach in Long Island Sound in Connecticut, and he'd fill his pockets with so many shells and beautiful rocks he found that his little shorts would be falling off him.

That evening, when I was about to enter the house, a woman called down to me from the third-floor window of our neighboring building.

"Excuse me, do you have a young son?"

I was a bit taken aback by her question. I knew she couldn't be referring to J.T., because he was practically as tall as I was. And of course, in my heart, I would always have a young son. I honestly didn't know how to answer, so I just pretended not to hear her. She asked again, this time more loudly.

"Do you have a young son?" When she saw me faltering, she added, "Because I saw you walking along the beach with him earlier today. I thought it was a beautiful picture."

I remembered that I had seen Trent, his wife Sasha, and young Hayden on the beach around sunset, and it had been such a Kodak moment that I actually did take a picture of them. I told the woman she must be mistaking me for my sister-in-law, who was walking with my nephew. "It wasn't me, but you're right, it was a beautiful picture," I shouted up to her.

She shook her head, certain that it was me she'd seen on the beach walking with my young son. Before she disappeared back through the window, she smiled at me and said, "*You* are beautiful!"

Being on the receiving end of such a random and sweet kindness warmed my heart. I have no idea who that woman was or if she happened to be clairvoyant, but when I thought over what she'd said, I knew she was right; she *had* seen Jesse walking along the beach with me. He may not be here physically, but he was with me in spirit. The woman's words reminded me of Mary Stevenson's beautiful poem "Footprints in the Sand," which tells us that even when we walk alone we can see two sets of footprints in the sand because Jesus is always walking at our side—and in our most difficult times, if we see only one set of footprints, it is because he is carrying us. The poem's tender imagery is such a powerful illustration of Jesus' compassion.

Compassion, I reminded myself, had to be at the very heart of the Choose Love Foundation, and it was time to move forward and build on this idea.

When I returned to Connecticut, my first goal was to find people who knew about teaching compassion and to ask them to help me develop programs for the foundation. And because I was ready, the teachers appeared. I asked Dr. Laura if she knew of anyone who taught compassion and she did—Professor Christopher Kukk at Western Connecticut State University. With a quick Google search I saw that Chris had been developing compassion-based curriculums for years, and had founded the Center for Compassion, Creativity and Innovation to promote compassion in universities. I rang him up immediately, and our first conversation lasted only 30 seconds as he was running out the door, but that was all the time I needed to tell him about my plans.

We clicked in an instant, like two souls coming

together to achieve a single purpose. When we met the following week in person at his campus office, I was even more convinced that we'd been brought together for a reason. He was working on compassion-themed school programs, writing children's books, and advocating for universities to adopt "Compassion Charters" as Spalding University in Kentucky had recently done in 2011. The idea was to create such a compassionate learning environment that the students graduated not only as top scholars but also as compassionate human beings. Chris had been a United States Army counterintelligence agent, he told me, and had seen what happened to people who were completely devoid of compassion, and how "dangerous and destructive" they could be.

We chatted nonstop for an hour; and when I stood up to leave, Chris had tears in his eyes.

"I am in this for the long haul," he said, hugging me good-bye. "I won't rest until we see a class of students graduating from college who began our program in kindergarten."

When I left Chris's office, I felt the same forceful, spiritual energy swirling around me as I had right after Jesse's funeral. It was an incredible, positive force of forward momentum, a feeling that great things were happening and about to happen. And they did, in rapid succession. I was invited along with other Sandy Hook parents to attend an upcoming speech that President Obama was to give at Hartford University, where he had set aside private one-on-one time to greet the parents before his speech. Then, I was asked to speak at a conference about reducing violence in schools, which was also to be held at Hartford University the day after the President's speech. I accepted both invitations as opportunities to spread Jesse's message and invited Chris, my new comrade-in-arms, to join me—our teamwork had begun!

When I discovered that the President's speech was to be on gun control, I told Chris on the phone that I'd rather skip it and remain focused on the compassion curriculum.

"Scarlett," he said, carefully, "let's think about this now. Your mission is to get nurturing, healing love heard and for it to become a part of our educational system, right? Now ask yourself, who is the one person that can help that happen?"

Chris was right; I had to take Jesse's message straight to the President.

Before President Obama gave his rousing, passionate, and convincing speech, Chris and I had a few minutes with him. It was just enough to give him a hug and launch into my pitch: "Hi, Mr. President, nice to see you again. I've started the Jesse Lewis Choose Love Foundation to bring compassion into our education system . . ."

I told the President about Jesse's messages and why I thought it was important for children to be taught compassion at an early age through school programs based on nurturing, healing love. He was completely focused on me and my words, nodding his head in agreement, saying, "Yes . . . *yes!*" Just like the first time I'd met him, he made me feel as though what I was saying mattered.

"We all have to choose love, Mr. President," I told him.

Chris Kukk and I have our first foundation "meeting" with President Obama

Chris took his cue and jumped in, giving the President details about the core curriculum and how it would work.

"Yes, *yes!*" the President said again. "I am totally on board with this. This is exactly what all our schools need to get across to every child in the country. This is important. I want you to talk to my sister because she's been working on exactly this kind of curriculum."

He turned to one of his assistants and told him to give us his sister Maya's phone number. "This is really important!" he repeated, to both his staff member and to us.

I couldn't believe what had just happened. It felt like . . . *victory!*

CHAPTER THIRTEEN

Message to the World

P resident Obama was good to his word and put Chris and me in touch with his sister Maya Soetoro-Ng, who was a kindred spirit and devoted to the same mission as us—helping to build a more compassionate world starting with our children.

We spoke to Maya from her home in Hawaii, where she runs her own compassion center, teaches courses at the University of Hawaii based on a compassion curriculum, and is working to bring compassion programs into all Hawaiian classrooms from kindergarten through grade 12.

"We call our curriculum the Seeds of Compassion," Maya said, explaining that the name was a tribute to the compassion initiatives of the Dalai Lama, whom she greatly admired. Who doesn't admire him? The Dalai Lama has dedicated his life to creating a more compassionate world. His own holistic blueprint for a compassionate global society is so well developed, intellectually sound, spiritually advanced, and scientifically researched that anyone (including me) designing a compassion-based program of any kind inevitably looks to the work of the Dalai Lama for guidance and inspiration.

Chris had met and worked with the Dalai Lama the year before at a conference he'd helped organize; he told me meeting the Dalai Lama was life changing for him. Maya, too, was about to meet the Dalai Lama as his honored guest at an upcoming peace symposium in Maryland. We talked about the Dalai Lama's level of commitment to raising the level of compassion across the planet, and then Maya expressed her own level of commitment to the Choose Love Foundation and the people of Newtown.

"I heard about Jesse . . . and everything that happened at Sandy Hook," she said to me. "I've been praying for a way to help you and the other families and children. I've been asking myself what can I do, and this is an answer to my prayer. Now I know. I'd like to be involved with the Foundation. I can help you. I am committed for life to helping you," she said.

Maya's passion, expertise, and kindness were like gifts handed to me, and they were soon followed up with another present. Because of a scheduling conflict, she was unable to attend the peace symposium in Maryland and offered me her "honored guest" tickets to see and meet the Dalai Lama in person!

I took J.T., my mom, and some friends including Lori and Dr. Laura with me to go see this inspiring spiritual leader, whose title means "Ocean Teacher." We were told when we arrived that scheduling made a face-to-face meeting with the Dalai Lama impossible. So, I sent up a little prayer to Jesse asking him to see what he could do from heaven to make it happen anyway. The following morning, before the event, I heard from

A man of compassion; a hug from the Dalai Lama

the Venerable Lama Tenzin Dhonden, co-founder of the Dalai Lama's compassion program: "I'm bringing the Dalai Lama to you in ten minutes."

He gave us instructions to wait in our hotel lobby, and so we waited, excited and nervous, on the main floor. Then I saw the Dalai Lama walking toward us, draped in burgundy cloth.

He bowed to us and shook J.T.'s hand. I quickly introduced him to my mom and Lori—then he looked at me with those remarkably soulful eyes, and I said, "I lost my son Jesse during the Sandy Hook tragedy."

"How old?" he asked softly.

"He was six," I answered.

He stepped toward me and embraced me tightly, gently cradling the back of my head with his strong right hand. It felt as though we stood like that forever. Lori told me later that she saw a tear roll down his cheek. My head tingled for the rest of the day; I can still feel it when I close my eyes and recall that miraculous moment.

During that weekend, while I was trying to absorb as much wisdom and knowledge as I could from him, I was struck by the thousands of hearts the Dalai Lama touched with his humble, self-effacing, and quietly passionate presentation.

Speaking publically was one way to get Jesse's message to the world, and I began to do this officially and in earnest the day after Chris and I spoke to the President at the University of Hartford, when I returned to Hartford to speak to a group on reducing violence in schools.

As I had done before, I spoke from the heart, telling

the audience that although Jesse's death could have destroyed me, hope, love, forgiveness, and faith had saved me. I welcomed the opportunity to speak about Jesse and his message and felt a responsibility to pass the message of nurturing, healing love along to others. But I didn't realize how deeply it would touch people and how much love I would receive in return.

When I finished speaking, every member of the audience lined up to hug me, most with tears in their eyes and all of them with their own story of grief that they wanted and needed to share—the aunt who was severely traumatized following the murder of her niece and nephew by their father; a mother whose little twin girls had been killed; the daughter whose mom was shot to death while sleeping in bed beside her; the loss of a loving grandparent. One by one, I listened to their stories, and then we hugged. It occurred to me that my own pain had been held up and displayed for the world to see for so many months that people were now able to identify with me through their own grief. But the wonderful upshot was that, like me, they were learning to reach out for help—and they were telling me that Jesse's "choose love" message was inspiring them to live more compassionate and happier lives.

If the Sandy Hook tragedy has taught me anything, it's that we are all united in our grief—and that love and compassion can heal and reshape both our hearts and our world, which was the theme of the next conference I was invited to speak at a few days later.

The Compassion Conference in Danbury, Connecticut, is an annual event sponsored by Chris's university, and it's where Chris met the Dalai Lama, who'd been the conference's keynote speaker the previous year. The gathering is dedicated to exploring ideas and methods that can help us practice compassion more effectively in our daily lives, and in our communities and institutions. So when Chris asked me to speak at the conference, I was flattered and jumped at the chance to contribute.

I was part of an education panel, and our group discussed how we could create more compassionate schools and cities by changing our thinking from a "me" to a "we" perspective, which is one of the Dalai Lama's teachings on compassion—building a world of oneness by shedding individual egos.

When I spoke, I shared Jesse's story as I always do, and then I said that I had seen the world shift its perspective from "me" to "we" on the day of the tragedy. "Everyone felt our pain that day; everyone felt like they had lost a child, or a brother or a sister or a friend." I described the beauty of the love letters and cards and gifts sent to us from people in practically every country on Earth—and how the warehouses in Newtown were still overflowing with hundreds of thousands of messages from total strangers who had taken the time to write.

"On that day the world became one; on that day the world chose love," I said. "But we have to keep that going through awareness and education. Nurturing, healing love—getting that message to the world is the reason Jesse was put on this Earth. He died for it."

Forty-eight hours later, two bombs were detonated at the Boston Marathon, seriously injuring dozens of people and killing three innocent souls, including an eight-year-old boy, who was standing just a few feet from one of the explosions. The boy's mother had been hurt, too, but she was alive and unconscious in the hospital. I worried for her, imagining the moment she'd wake up and be told by someone that her son was gone.

I travelled to Boston the next day to visit my brother Coulter and his family—and that little boy and his mother were still very much on my mind. I visited the Louis D. Brown Peace Institute in Dorchester, Massachusetts, where that sweet boy was from. The institute is headed by Tina Chéry, whose son had been gunned down 17 years earlier on a Boston street as he was on his way to an antiviolence Christmas party. Tina had helped me through my anguish in the months following Jesse's death, and now she was busy helping those affected by the Boston bombings. As I rushed for a taxi I caught sight of a picture of the little boy who had just died on the front page of a newspaper as I passed a newsstand—it was a photo of him standing in his classroom, holding up a blue cardboard sign on which he'd used colored markers to write the message "No more hurting people. Peace."

And he'd drawn little hearts and a peace sign around the words.

I couldn't believe my eyes! It reminded me so much of Jesse's nurturing, healing love. I was tingling from head to toe with the sense of spiritual "knowing" I got whenever Jesse sent me a sign. I thought, *I wonder if the boys are in on this together.* The little boy in Boston was two years older than Jesse, his spelling was definitely better, and the words were slightly different, but the sentiment expressed by both of them was exactly the same. "No more hurting people. Peace" and "Nurturing, healing love"—the message is identical.

But how long will it take to get this message to the world? How many other children will have to die before we wake up, before we make room in our hearts and in our schools for compassion—before we all learn to choose love?

Help me, Jesse, I prayed. *Help me to reach the world with your message.*

Two days later, President Obama arrived to console the victims of the Boston bombing, just as he had done in Sandy Hook to console us four months earlier. And as he had done in Sandy Hook, he spoke publically about what had been done and what we had to do in response.

And, oh, I wanted to hug him at that moment—and I wanted to cry. Because what the President of the United States of America chose to say to the people of Boston, words that would be broadcast to people around the world, could not have been more perfect.

It was our mantra, it was our hope, and it was the answer to my prayer.

And neither Jesse nor I would have said it any differently, or could have said it any better than the President:

> You showed us, Boston, that in the face of evil, Americans will lift up what's good.
>
> In the face of cruelty, we will choose compassion.
>
> In the face of those who would visit death upon innocents, we will choose to save, and to comfort, and to heal.
>
> We'll choose friendship.
>
> *We'll choose love.*

Love Never Ends

One May morning something shifted inside of me.

I woke up and the sun was shining and I went upstairs and did something I thought I'd never do again: I picked up a brush, dipped it into color, and began to paint. My easel held the unfinished portrait I'd last been working on—one of Jesse on a dock in Maine, blowing bubbles toward the August sky. I gently began brushing in details to his face, his hair.

The early spring had been difficult; Jesse loved to splash around in the thawing mud and watch the birds return from the south. Part of me wanted to stay frozen in winter, when he died, but something else pulled my heart toward the sunshine.

And now I wanted to create again, to paint, which is something I've loved to do since childhood and hadn't done since December.

It's now been six months since Jesse's left this Earth; and of course, I have many days when I still struggle—some days more than others. There are moments when I don't choose love, when I can't, when it's too difficult for me. And that's okay, too. I know I'll have other opportunities to do so and that changing one's way of thinking is an ongoing, long-term process.

As any parent who has lost a child will tell you, there is no overnight remedy for the heartache. What I have learned, and what I have done my best to share with you throughout these pages, is that with the help and love of others, and with faith, hope, and time, healing is possible. Things improve, and one day it feels like life is worth living again, we can smile again, and we can laugh. At least, that's what is happening for me.

The mornings are still painful, but not as bad. Through my many forms of healing therapy I've learned how to "schedule" time for my grief, which is before noon most days, when I visit the cemetery. I spend 15 minutes at Jesse's grave—I say the Lord's Prayer, I touch his tombstone, I tell him how sorry I am, I thank him for all the signs he sends us, and I cry. With this done, I'm able to carry on and do what I must do with composure and the ability find joyful moments throughout the day. And most important, I am able to be present, strong, and positive for J.T.

It's beautiful now at the grave site; we have a stone bench and a bluebird house and birdbath where a little family of Jesse's ducks is always swimming. There's the rosebush and pink star dogwood that Mom and I planted together on Mother's Day; and, of course, on constant patrol in front of Jesse's tombstone is his platoon of army men. I bring Jesse a new little toy every few days from the collection of gifts sent to us by the people who reached out in love from around the world. We have so many, and I know how Jesse loved to share, so I often visit the graves of the other

Jesse's grave stone, lined with his little rubber ducks

children who were taken from us that day and leave
each one a little present as well.

Some days I just lie on the bench and look up
through the leaves of the oak tree that shelters the site
and tell Jesse about my day, about everything J.T. is
up to, and how work on his Choose Love Foundation
is progressing. And lately the news has been so, so
great.

J.T. and I are in a better place. We read together
every night, and he's working hard on raising money
to send more Rwandan orphans to college. As a
Mother's Day gift, he came to Boston with me to join
thousands of other families who lost loved ones to
violence and walk in the 14th annual Louis D. Brown
Mother's Day Walk for Peace. I talk a lot about how
brave and strong Jesse was, but I look at J.T. and think
he is the essence of both physical and mental strength,

too. He has developed this might, honing it through trial and refining it by fire. I am so proud of him.

Jesse's Choose Love Foundation is coming together in ways I had only dreamed possible—we have a dedicated, passionate, and extremely capable board of directors; many caring and knowledgeable advisors have volunteered to help us; there is growing support and backing from our friends, family, educators, and politicians; and we have a great new website and a fledgling fund-raising campaign.

My mission keeps me focused and moving forward— I'm in it for life and won't stop until I can report to Jesse: *Mission accomplished!*

But there's still a lot of work to be done. And Jesse is always by my side, continuing to send me signs and help every day. And I thank him every day, saying, "You've done a great job of putting the pieces together for us down here and taking care of your family. We are all okay. We miss you so much, baby!"

Lately during our visits together, I've been telling Jesse all about the plans for his upcoming seventh birthday, on June 30. I've invited 500 people to celebrate his amazing life, including our family, our oldest and dearest friends, Jesse's playmates, as well our new friends and family—the first responders, police officers, firefighters, my Healing Hearts family, foundation friends, and so many others, like Trooper Rob and Dr. Laura, whose love and support have carried us through.

Jesse will love the party, which we'll start with a small family gathering in the morning at the cemetery where Trent will sing a song he composed in Jesse's honor called "Waiting for Our Wings." We'll toast our sweet boy with champagne, and then set off dozens of balloons.

After that, it's off to Zoar Ridge Stables to greet Jesse's guests and begin the rest of the day's celebration with a big barbeque, live music, and plenty of activities to make sure that Jesse's little cousins and young friends will "have a lot of fun"—pony rides, face painting, a magician, swimming, and a giant water slide.

Yesterday, I delivered party invitations to the firehouse, which had been the center of such trauma and pain on the day of the shooting. But walking through the building now didn't throw me into a panic or traumatize me at all. As I left the firehouse, I looked up at the roof at the 26 recently installed copper stars glowing in the sun and saw Jesse's star was front and center, as if to say, *Heeeeeeere's Jesse!*

Then later, back at home, I did something else I hadn't done since the tragedy; I went into the barn and saddled up Heart, our horse whose mother was Rose of *Rose's Foal*. I love horseback riding as passionately as I love painting. I thought both of those loves had been lost to me forever when I lost Jesse, but now I know they aren't because I haven't really lost Jesse. He's with me wherever I am—flying in a jet to Florida, strolling along a distant beach, on a New York stage addressing thousands of people, or trying to convince the President of the United States the importance of teaching Jesse's message in our schools. He's beside me always, all the way, and always will be. Love never ends.

As I rode Heart across the fields behind the farm, I smelled the sweet wildflowers just coming into bloom and felt the warmth of the sun on my face. I looked up at the clear blue sky and realized that, at least for that moment, I was happy.

And that was the best sign I've received so far. Thank you, my precious Jesse.

Love never ends . . .

Acknowledgments

FROM SCARLETT

I want to thank my beautiful family for holding me up during the dark night of my soul—caring for me and comforting me with incredible generosity of spirit and unconditional love I never thought possible—Trent and Sasha Lewis, Jordan and Becky Lewis, and Coulter and Kristy Lewis.

I want to thank my mom, Maureen Lewis, and my stepfather, Bob Comfort, for opening their home for weeks on end to an endless group of friends and for attending difficult meetings and working out the details in the background.

I want to thank my dad, David Lewis, for his help with the foundation and his wife, Beth Mack, for her loving acts of kindness and support.

Thank you to all the friends who supported my family and, in turn, me.

I want to thank Dr. Laura Asher, who took my hand during those first few weeks and walked me through blinding despair and into the light. She continues to nurture me along my journey.

Thank you, Trooper Rob Maurice, who was our guardian angel during those first few weeks and who will forevermore be part of our family.

I thank my neighbors Chan and Roberta Ahuja and their sons for demonstrating Christlike consciousness in their daily lives.

Thank you to Pastor Richard Flashman, who opened his church and his heart and tirelessly shared the words of our Lord.

Also thanks to our precious Marissa Bonjourno and her mother, Susan, for being a part of God's Master Plan and such dear friends to Jesse.

To Dave and Michele Foster and their kids (the youngest of whom I have recently become a Godmother to!) and John Merkowitz for stepping up to the plate when I needed it most.

Thanks to Barbara Ross, who coordinated help for my animals and so much more and has been a friend since I purchased her farm!

Thank you to my precious girlfriends from Darien High School who came from all over the country to be by my side when I buried my precious Jesse.

Thank you Carol Gormin, my first friend in Connecticut and one of my most valiant supporters, and Missy Fiorita who has always been there.

Thank you to Diane Alena for more than I can say.

Thank you to all my friends who came to Jesse's wake and funeral, and who now support the foundation—I know who you are and I love you, too.

Thank you, thank you, thank you to Robert and Colleen Haines, who helped get the foundation off the ground and running, as well as lovingly and tirelessly planning Jesse's birthday party and making it a special healing day for so many.

Thank you to Maureen Clark and Jan Stabile, two angels who swooped down to help save me.

Thank you Julie Sanders for 41 years—and counting—of friendship.

Thank you to Trout and Jennifer Gaskins, who sacrificed days and days to provide friendship and comfort and even baby lambs on Christmas Eve!

Thank you Linda Couch for being a source of inspiration for me throughout my life and showing me that we have the strength and courage to face our greatest challenges.

Thank you to Pam and Mike Blasko for always being there for us with selfless love and for going above and beyond, and to Ashly and Rick Bartholomew for loving us with childlike abandon.

Thank you to Diana Simpson and my dear stepson, David Burke, for their never-ending love and support.

Thank you to Nick Ortner, who is one of the truest people I know, for providing me with a method of relief that has stayed with me. And thank you to Dr. Lori Leydon for intuitively helping our family navigate our pain and frustration and move to peace.

Thank you to Rob and Debora Accomando of My Sandy Hook Family Fund for their integrity and their faithful, unwavering support of the victim's families.

Thank you to my community for their continued loving support.

Thanks to Wayne Dyer for recognizing and experiencing how special Jesse's spirit continues to be, and to

Having fun at the farmer's market

Louise Hay, whose teachings enabled me to be present for Jesse and have few regrets.

Thank you to Patty Gift and the entire Hay House staff for your understanding and belief in this book's message.

It is with such gratitude that I thank Natasha Stoynoff, whom I am convinced was handpicked by Jesse to help write this book. The synchronicities we have experienced during this project could fill another book!

And thank you to Natasha's wonderful husband, Steve. I was miraculously doubly blessed with his incredible insight, knowledge, and sweet support—whatever you say goes. I will forever cherish the special rosary you gave me; thank you for completing the circle of love.

Thank you world, adults and children alike, for your loving messages, handmade gifts of such poignant sweetness, and, most of all, continued prayers.

I am grateful to God and his son, Jesus Christ, who are the basis of my strength and courage.

Thank you, Mother Mary, for showing your presence, knowing my suffering, and providing me with an example of how to continue in grace.

Most of all, thank you to my precious son J.T., who taught me the meaning of love when he was born and continues to be my greatest teacher.

And lastly . . . thank you to Jesse, who continues to send me nurturing, healing love from beyond—keep the signs coming! XO

FROM NATASHA

First and foremost, an immeasurable thank-you to Steve—whose creativity, heart, and smarts helped make this book.

A big kiss goes to the ever-fantabulous gang at Hay House—Patty, Laura, Shannon, and Reid.

Thank you to Wayne and Nick, for being the first to recognize the beauty of Scarlett's story.

A heartfelt thank-you to pretty Miss Maureen, our gentle reader and my personal cheerleader. Love to Scarlett's entire family, who welcomed me into the circle as their own.

To J.T.—the coolest teen and my future co-Oscar-winner—thanks for taking good care of your mom and me as we worked!

For my dear, sweet sister-in-law, Miss Melly, who acted as agent from the Other Side and delivered me directly into Scarlett's hands with her own—*after all . . . tomorrow . . .*

And thank you to JE, for confirming the Big Sign.

To Maria and Vasily, please take care of Jesse as you did and do me.

And to my dearest Miss Scarlett, my new Southern soul sister and sharer of my special moniker: Thank you for trusting me to roam around inside your heart and help you with your mission. You amaze me.

And last—but never least, and always with us—thank you, Jesse. Meet me by the bubble bath, I've got the ducks all lined up . . .

Wearing his winter "army" boots on a hot summer day, June 2012

ABOUT THE AUTHORS

Scarlett Lewis is a mother, artist, avid horsewoman and a new activist for peace. She is the founder of *The Jesse Lewis Choose Love Foundation*, created in honour of her son who was killed in the Sandy Hook Elementary School massacre in December 2012. Scarlett graduated from Boston University with a BS in Communications and has worked as a writer and in finance. In 2007, she wrote and illustrated the children's book, *Rose's Foal*, about a foal born on her farm and the important life lessons his mother taught him. Scarlett lives with her family on a farm in Newtown, Connecticut.

Natasha Stoynoff is a *New York Times* best-selling author and former staff writer for *People* and freelancer for *Time* magazines. She lives in Manhattan, where she is currently working on books, screenplays and her first off-Broadway play.

www.jesselewischooselove.org

ABOUT the FOUNDATION

The mission of the Jesse Lewis Choose Love Foundation is to create awareness in our children and our communities that we can choose love over anger, gratitude over entitlement, and forgiveness and compassion over bitterness. Our goal is to create a more peaceful and loving world through planting these seeds of wisdom. We are dedicated to working with any group or person who shares our goals, and the Board is dedicated to maximizing every investment in this partnership to further the mission of the Foundation.

To learn more about or make a donation to the Jesse Lewis Choose Love Foundation, please visit www.jesselewischooselove.org.

HAY HOUSE TITLES OF RELATED INTEREST

YOU CAN HEAL YOUR LIFE, the movie,
starring Louise L. Hay & Friends
(available as a 1-DVD programme and an expanded 2-DVD set)
Watch the trailer at: **www.LouiseHayMovie.com**

THE SHIFT, the movie,
starring Dr. Wayne W. Dyer
(available as a 1-DVD programme and
an expanded 2-DVD set)
Watch the trailer at: **www.DyerMovie.com**

CHANGE YOUR THOUGHTS, CHANGE YOUR LIFE:
Living the Wisdom of the Tao, by Dr Wayne W. Dyer

LEFT TO TELL: One Woman's Story of Surviving the Rwandan
Holocaust, by Immaculée Ilibagiza

THE RADICAL PRACTICE OF LOVING EVERYONE:
A Four-Legged Approach to Enlightenment,
by Michael Chase

THE TAPPING SOLUTION: A Revolutionary System for Stress-
Free Living, by Nick Ortner

**All of the above are available at your local bookstore,
or may be ordered by contacting Hay House
(see next page).**

We hope you enjoyed this Hay House book. If you'd like to receive our online catalogue featuring additional information on Hay House books and products, or if you'd like to find out more about the Hay Foundation, please contact:

Hay House UK, Ltd., Astley House, 33 Notting Hill Gate, London W11 3JQ
Phone: 0-20-3675-2450 • *Fax:* 0-20-3675-2451
www.hayhouse.co.uk • **www.hayfoundation.org**

Published and distributed in Australia by: Hay House Australia Pty. Ltd., 18/36 Ralph St., Alexandria NSW 2015 • *Phone:* 612-9669-4299
Fax: 612-9669-4144 • www.hayhouse.com.au

Published and distributed in the United States by: Hay House, Inc., P.O. Box 5100, Carlsbad, CA 92018-5100
Phone: (760) 431-7695 or (800) 654-5126
Fax: (760) 431-6948 or (800) 650-5115
www.hayhouse.com®

Published and distributed in the Republic of South Africa by: Hay House SA (Pty), Ltd., P.O. Box 990, Witkoppen 2068 • *Phone/Fax:* 27-11-467-8904
www.hayhouse.co.za

Published in India by: Hay House Publishers India, Muskaan Complex, Plot No. 3, B-2, Vasant Kunj, New Delhi 110 070 • *Phone:* 91-11-4176-1620
Fax: 91-11-4176-1630 • www.hayhouse.co.in

Distributed in Canada by: Raincoast, 9050 Shaughnessy St., Vancouver, B.C. V6P 6E5 • *Phone:* (604) 323-7100 • *Fax:* (604) 323-2600 • www.raincoast.com

TAKE YOUR SOUL ON A VACATION

Visit **www.HealYourLife.com**® to regroup, recharge, and reconnect with your own magnificence.
Featuring blogs, mind-body-spirit news, and life-changing wisdom from Louise Hay and friends.

Visit **www.HealYourLife.com** today!

Free e-newsletters from Hay House, the Ultimate Resource for Inspiration

Be the first to know about Hay House's dollar deals, free downloads, special offers, affirmation cards, giveaways, contests, and more!

 Get exclusive excerpts from our latest releases and videos from *Hay House Present Moments*.

 Enjoy uplifting personal stories, how-to articles, and healing advice, along with videos and empowering quotes, within *Heal Your Life*.

 Have an inspirational story to tell and a passion for writing? Sharpen your writing skills with insider tips from *Your Writing Life*.

Sign Up Now!

Get inspired, educate yourself, get a complimentary gift, and share the wisdom!

http://www.hayhouse.com/newsletters.php

Visit www.hayhouse.com to sign up today!

HealYourLife.com ♥